GENERATIVE FATHERING

Engaging fathers in family based programs

ANDREW KING
DR JOSEPH FLEMING
AND MOHAMED DUKULY

Generative Fathering: Engaging fathers into family based programs - Andrew King, Dr Joseph Fleming and Mohamed Dukuly
ISBN 978-0-6480015-5-3 (Paperback)
ISBN 978-0-6480015-7-7 (eBook)

Published by
Groupwork Solutions
Ph: 0437 546 560
E-mail: info@groupworksolutions.com.au
www.groupworksolutions.com.au

Cover and interior design by Amie McCracken
Cover image from altanaka

Sub editing: Tara Hunt and Graham Kettlewell

REVIEWS

"This is a very good guide for professionals working with fathers across many health and welfare settings. It walks new pathways that encourage men to be included in family interventions and provides many useful examples of how it can be done. This approach may seem obvious but past research has shown that men are frequently ignored. The book begins with a review of recent theory and research into working with men and then progresses to a guide as to how to proceed. It is clearly written and easy for professionals to understand; it gives case examples illustrating all types of problems, professional interventions and outcomes. Such material shows exactly what the authors mean and demonstrates the value of authors with extensive professional experience in working with men, especially in their parenting role".

Professor Emeritus Thea Brown, Department of Social Work, Monash University

"The social awareness that fathers play a crucial role in children's lives is often discussed in the negative. That is, how fathers are too absent, how they may harm their families through violence or dominance, or discussions about power and social inequity. It is true that as a society we have much to address, however we also need to look at how we meaningfully engage men through their own positive intent and capacity, and to understand more fully the barriers to greater contributions. This excellent book is strengths based and offers service providers an opportunity to critique their own work with fathers and the generative possibilities that men contribute to their children's lives. This book is timely and offers an important and unique perspective on men as fathers in contemporary society".

Elisabeth Shaw, CEO, Relationships Australia NSW

"A richly informative book which brilliantly makes the case for including fathers in family-work and offers a wealth of tips and strategies for doing so. The chapters on engaging with separated fathers, culturally diverse fathers, fathers of children with special needs and fathers who use violence are especially remarkable. We'll definitely be drawing on this book in our work."

Adrienne Burgess, Joint CEO, the Fatherhood Institute. www.fatherhoodinstitute.org

"This book is really good and easy to read. I think that the issues of fathers are often overlooked by professionals as we have traditionally been mostly women seeing mothers. The book also helps men/fathers to have clarity around their role in a changing society. Men need other men to tell them it is normal to want to look after their children. Men and women need to support men to participate in the nurturing of their children. This also leads to better support for women (as you have outlined) and further moves our society towards gender equality. It's great to have a bloke's perspective that is aligned with other gender equality texts".

Janelle Clifton, Occupational Therapist, Western Australia.

About Andrew King

Andrew King is a leading group work specialist in community services, counselling and health. A respected author of multiple text books and training programs, he has devoted a large part of his career to group work and working with men, fathering and domestic violence.

As a research practitioner Andrew is known for his focus on generativity and sharing his knowledge using a strengths-based approach. He has published a range of articles on group work leadership in the Australian context and facilitates national and international training workshops. He is the author of several recent books - Engaging men's responses to family violence (2017) and Continual Change Groupwork (2018). Andrew is currently the Practice Specialist, Groupwork and Community Education Manager at Relationships Australia, NSW. He is a father of two daughters.

About Dr Joe Fleming

Dr Fleming has over 25 years of experience in social work practice in Australia. He has a special interest in working with people and communities that are often described as 'hard to reach or engage'. Joe is passionate about research and is a published author and has presented at numerous seminars and conferences. He is a co-author of a chapter titled: Recruiting and Engaging Men as Fathers in Social Work Practice, by Peck and Cargill (2015). Dr Fleming is currently a registered mental health social worker and casual academic and also working in regional areas in WA the NT and NSW.

About Mohamed Dukuly

Mohamed Dukuly is a psychosocial educator, a social worker and an accredited Family Dispute Resolution practitioner. He currently works with migrants and refugees in Australia. He was born in Liberia and later migrated to Nigeria in the late 1990s and moved to Australia in 2005. He holds a Degree in Education and postgraduate qualifications in Social Science and Family Mediation and a Master of Social Work (professional qualifying).

TABLE OF CONTENTS

LIST OF FIGURES

LIST OF TABLES

PREFACE

The preface is one of the most important parts of any book to read. For this book, the preface provides an all-important insight into our motivation to develop the ideas and concepts central to our work. Each of us are informed by our diverse life experiences, be it lifelong practice in social services, growing up in working-class communities, the flight across countries and borders as a refugee, supporting parents with special needs, being a father, step-father or other lifelong commitments, or building communities in which we identify with or live. Despite these varying experiences we come together united through the practice of generativity using a variety of relational, developmental, spiritual and ethical practices.

We wrote this book primarily for practitioners who have an interest or curiosity in working with fathers. The initial chapters of this book present a strengths-based (often called a non-deficit) approach as the gold-standard framework through which to engaging fathers in family based programs. It builds on decades of practice in managing fathers' centres, supporting other fathers programs throughout Australia, working in mental health contexts to working in culturally diverse or isolated Aboriginal communities and engaging young people at risk of dropping out of school and society. Converging evidence supports the importance of strengths-based approaches to engaging fathers, yet the practice literature provides minimal guidance on how these approaches can be implemented in practice.

We believe this practice gap can be filled by the framework of generativity, which is presented in the second half of *Generative Fathering*. Generativity refers to the sacrificial caring or support provided to a significant relationship or the next generation, and evidence of it can be found throughout all societies. The generative motivation can be found in a variety of activities including child rearing, community gardening, caring for animals, mentoring others and volunteering. Arguably, generativity is a measure of our capacity to support and care for one another and is a fundamental backbone in any functional society. Generativity is summed up in the idea that when we give we receive back more than we gave in return.

The concept of generativity was first linked to working with fathers by Andrew Chudleigh, an Australian community development worker who had a vision to enhance family well-being through the development of a fathers' centre. Andrew's initial passion for a generativity-oriented fathers' centre had a profound impact on many others in the Australian community services field including us, the authors. Ericson's original concept of generativity is located within stages of psychosocial development. Within this framework, generativity was the key to maintaining integrity versus giving in to despair when exposed to the challenges of aging. Along the way, the original concept of generativity many would have been exposed to in Psychology 101 was further developed by Alan Hawkins, David Dollahite, Sean Brotherson, John Snarey and George Vaillant, as well as many others. These researchers applied generativity to the research of fathering, health and well-being that continues to have an impact today through the context of positive psychology. Ross Fletcher was a separated father's worker at a fathers' centre in Sydney who intuitively understood the practice of generativity and applied it successfully to working with separated fathers. This demonstrates an invaluable transition between theoretical and practical toolsets.

To ensure the best flow of ideas, *Generative Fathering* uses a plain English style rather than an academic one. We have also preferred to use endnotes to acknowledge the origins of ideas rather than using standard referencing practice throughout. The ideas contained in the book extend on themes and issues that we have developed and published in peer reviewed journal articles over the last two decades.

We all have a different story about fathering and generativity

Andrew King

I initially learned about sacrifice and care from my father who was my mother's carer. Being the youngest child, and the last to leave the house, I learnt intimately about the importance of caring and generativity (and the use of empathy). Yet as a father, his desire to fix situations for his children's sake was often at odds with the generative support that they required. To be truly generative you need allow your young adult children to grow up independently, self-sufficiently and stand on their own two feet. It is only through these ethical reflections that the best decisions can be made.

It is this letting-go aspect of love, that is completely different to giving off or being invisible, that is often the hardest, yet most generative act, a father can do. It is important to be there when needed but also to allow your child to develop their own self-survival skills to life, love and care for self and others. No doubt, many women struggle with this. Many fathers talk about this aspect of parenting less, hence, this book is one important way to voice the significance and importance of the generative role in men's lives. I thank my wife Rhonda, for her support and love over these many years. I have learnt more from watching her ability to impart generativity to our children than all other experiences. I greatly appreciate her patience and support that allowed me to write this book.

Dr Joe Fleming

In my early years I formed a personal view that fathers do not matter, as my mother raised my twin sister and I as a single parent. I only recall fleeting moments of quasi "father figures" in my life but none could measure up to the task of truly being a father as I had thought it to be from popular fiction, such as Atticus Finch from Harper Lee's "To Kill a Mockingbird". In the book Atticus conducts himself with dignity as he shares important moral lessons with his children, Jem and Scout.

However for the most part, fathers are often given a bad reputation in novels, films and advertising; they are absent, ineffectual, or the source of a lifetime's worth of psychological problems. Yet, there are some good ones out there, and my view changed later in life. As I started to try and understand why fathers were absent I developed an uncontrollable curiosity which led me onto further post-graduate studies and eventually contributing to the research base on fathers in child and family welfare practice. I thank my family and professional colleagues for encouraging me to dig deeper into the meaning of the word 'father' and especially Andrew King who in many ways has taught me to keep on digging.

Mohamed Dukuly

Coming to Australia brought about a significant change in my professional role and life experiences. When you face these changes as a Culturally and Linguistically Diverse (CALD) father there are few opportunities to talk it through with someone who fully understands the complexity of what we are going through. Through participating in writing this book, it provides the community health, counselling sector guidance on how to appropriately engage CALD fathers – especially when trauma issues are involved. It is my also my hope that this book will not only assist practitioners but CALD fathers as well to better understand their motivation and life journey.

CHAPTER 1:

WHY CONSIDER FATHERS

'Fatherhood is no simple phenomenon, but a complex tapestry of many things...the reality [is] that fatherhood is not a static phenomenon, but more like a moving target, only some of which has constant meaning'[1].

The role of fathers is changing, yet these developments have largely not been reflected in community service practice. This chapter presents the rationale behind including fathers in community, social work, psychology, counselling, domestic violence and health services. This chapter highlights how these diverse contexts have struggled to include men and fathers in the past.

The term 'father' is used to identify a social, rather than biological relationship. As a result, some of this information is relevant to non-biological fathers, mothers, and lesbian, gay, bisexual and transgender couples. The authors take the position that every person has the capacity to be an excellent and effective parent, and fathers need to be given the opportunity to be involved in their children's lives. In fact, the growing diversity of people's life course and the residency patterns for men and children has fostered a new awareness of the diversity of both mothers' and fathers' roles in contemporary society. Many of the tools used in this guide can also be applied to working with fathers in gay relationships or are very similar to those tools used when working with women from marginalised communities.

The changing role of fathers

The timeless question of the 'chicken and the egg' is a great metaphor for parenting our children. What came first, the adult or the child? Do children make great parents or do parents make great children? Over many generations, most cultures developed with traditional role expectations for men to be the 'hunters and gatherers' and women the 'nurturers and carers' who support families. In the past, both parents had concrete expectations of the role they played in the family, their relationship, and the broader community.

The traditional role of men in the past has created a challenge for all fathers, especially those who become divorced or separated. In the past, men have usually increased their involvement in parenting as the children get older and developed more cognitive and gross motor skill ability (i.e. to play sport). However, currently more fathers[2] are involved in the immediate care of the children as babies and throughout their development than ever before[3]. After World War II, 5% of men attended the birth of their children[4]. In the 1980's, it was estimated that 80% of men were attending the birth of their children. Today, male partners attend 98% of births in industrialised countries[5;6]. Further, the number of dads using flexible working arrangements to care for their children has doubled since the mid-90s. Around 30% of dads took advantage of flexible work hours to look after young children (under 12), compared with 16% of dads two decades ago. The number of dads being the primary carer of their children doubled from 7 per cent to 14 per cent, while dads who worked part-time to allow them to care for their children rose from 1 per cent to 5 per cent[7]. These changes have forged a movement that means men today father very differently to how they were fathered. In 1999, the Australian Government conducted research into the role fathers were playing in family relationships[8]. It identified that for many men, their relationship with their children is a very significant connection in their life.

Benefits of having fathers more involved with their children

Leading researchers and studies, both internationally and in Australia, have identified that being an involved father brings with it many health and social benefits to fathers and children[9].

The benefits of fathers' involvement are:
- Experienced by the father - When fathers build strong relationships with their children and others in the family they are more likely to receive support and caring in return. Healthy family relationships

provide the strongest and most important support network a person can have, whether that person is a child or an adult. Active involvement in family life helps fathers enjoy a secure attachment relationship with their children, enhances resiliency to cope with stressful situations and everyday hassles, feel more comfortable in their occupation and feel that they can do their job well, and feel confident they have a lot to offer others in terms of their job skills, parenting skills, and social relationship[10].

- Experienced by the mother – As long as conflict does not regularly exist in the family, the mother will experience higher levels of support and reductions in stress.
- Experienced by the children - Research also shows that there is an association between fathers' early involvement in a child's life and early educational achievement, positive parent-child relationships in adolescence, and protection from mental health problems in the context of separated families[11].

Other benefits for the children include improved cognitive competence in infants, higher academic achievement in school aged children, and increased likelihood of positive peer relations among adolescents[12].

Challenges to get fathers involved

There are multiple reasons that fathers may be less involved in health and child welfare services[13]. Barriers include:

- Competing use of resources that are time-restricted and cannot be delivered outside of normal working hours;
- Assumptions made by the health and child welfare systems that do not include, or can actively exclude, the involvement of the fathers;
- Mothers who are unwilling to include the father, or do not identify the father to service providers ;
- Threats of domestic violence in current or past relationships;
- Practitioners who traditionally focus child welfare interventions upon mothers and children, and fathers regarded as a parent adjunct[14];
- Practitioners who lack the knowledge or skills to involve fathers, especially with vulnerable families; and,
- Fathers who view parenting as the mother's role, or find that interventions are not focused upon their perceived needs or preferred activities, and consequently avoid contact with practitioners.

Parent-education groups often have more mothers accessing the programs than fathers, despite the provision of group, couple, or individual learning opportunities. Whilst not all fathers will attend parenting education programs, it is important that these fathers are not labelled as 'hard-to-reach', as this is unlikely to increase engagement with services. Some of the ways in which services and practitioners can overcome this issue with fathers will be discussed in Chapter 5, under the section *Principles for effective practice.*

Common views of fathering in the community services

Comprehension of the role fathers play in postmodern society is still in its infancy within both the community services and the general media. The role has significantly changed due to lower marriage rates, new reproductive technologies, and political consequences of the second-wave feminist movement[15]. The evolution of the fathering role and the flow on effect to the varying attitude, behaviours, and discourses of social welfare professionals has impacted the involvement of fathers in social services. This is particularly evident in the legal frameworks and diverse institutional practices developed since the post-war decades of the 1950s and the 1960s[16,17,18]. In child protection and family welfare settings, abusers who are fathers are particularly visible. Professionals struggle to see fathers as resources, even those who are not the abusers and wish to care for their children (when the mother is unable to care for them)[19,20,21].

Community-service practice often focuses on mothers and their narratives, as they have been most commonly seen in child welfare practice[22,23,24,25,26,27,28]. There is no shortage of research to suggest that fathers tend to be avoided by professionals, and possibly vice versa – amid great uncertainty about how to approach fathers and work with them effectively [29,30,31]. The reviewed research highlights that child and family welfare services are often slow to adapt to the changing realities of family life and even slower to take an active role in promoting change in families, particularly in the area of child protection [32,33,34]. Scourfield identified how men and women clients were constructed differently in child protection work[35]. In his ethnographic study, he recognised that notions of masculinity, femininity, and family experience are socially constructed. Even though the assessment of men is essential when there are allegations of physical or sexual abuse, the generalised portrayal of all men as a threat is problematic. The mother in the relationship is often expected to make a choice between her partner and the child or children. If she did not make this choice, this was viewed by professionals as her failing to protect herself or her children. Rigid constructions of masculinity and femininity are detrimental to community work practice and require revision to facilitate the engagement of fathers in family-based practice.

Practitioners' support of families may be impaired by the adoption of inflexible perspectives of fathers. An analysis of case reviews into the deaths or serious injuries of children where abuse or neglect were known or suspected found a tendency for professionals to adopt what they term 'rigid' or 'fixed' thinking about the father[36]. Fathers were labelled as either 'all good' or 'all bad'. This sort of assessment resulted in the father's value being less visible and not regarded seriously as of benefit to the children, even when they have not been violent towards the children or the mother. The consequences of diametric labelling prevented practitioners from taking the views expressed by 'bad fathers' seriously and it was difficult for practitioners to balance fathers' ability to change alongside past patterns of behaviour.

The view of fathers within the community services needs to be broadened to encompass the evolution of the concept of masculinity, fatherhood, and the dual roles fathers are now expected to fulfil. Research suggests that although fathers today spend more time caring for their children than they did a few decades ago[37], many men continue to feel the role of breadwinning is the key to being a "good father"[38]. The obligation to meet these dual roles in a new social context not demanded historically has resulted in men reporting an increasing level of conflict between their work and family demands[39,40]. Once work and family were thought to be separate social spheres. They are now viewed as interconnected[41,42].

Understanding how fathers' work and family-role experiences are connected can importantly inform professionals about how to better accommodate all their clients, not just mothers. Integrating work and family roles is an issue relevant to all professionals; it is not solely a women's issue. An example of this is in the Australian mining industry, which has seen an increase in employment for both men and women. Employment in the mining industry brings substantial economic gain for men and women. However miners can face a number of stressors on the job, including long work hours, rotating shifts, time away from family and children and risks from the work including death[43], all of which place them at a higher risk for negative parenting outcomes. The occupational conditions inherent within the mining industry have only recently emerged as problematic for practitioners and their families[44,45].

Whilst there is an emerging trend internationally to increase understanding of modern fatherhood[46,47,48], there has been little research on men's experience of fatherhood undertaken in Australia. Collier and Sheldon argue that decades of social, cultural and legal change mean that fatherhood is open-ended, fluid and fragmented[49]. The lives of men cannot be comprehended through the deployment of binaries of good and bad dads, and new and traditional fathers. Moreover, they argue that 'traditional fatherhood' is persistent in its continued hold over social and cultural expectations of fathers, making the tensions for some men to choose between employment breadwinner roles versus family and childcare commitments. Their framework of fragmenting fatherhood is useful to professionals and other professionals in this respect, as it offers up a new way of seeing fathers beyond the traditional frame of reference. Effective engagement strategies to not only invite fathers in to services but also keep them involved are required. Relationships between parents and practitioners play a greater role during the period of early childhood development than at any other time in a child's life [50,51]. As a result, practitioners need to support the involvement and engagement of men as an active agent in their children's lives.

Research suggests that despite the practice issues that function as barriers to father involvement, generally practitioners are keen to work with fathers in their service. The central practice dilemma that consistently emerges from the research is how to include fathers who are described by professionals as being physically absent, non-resident or have abusive social histories. In these situations it was often the professionals that appeared not to have necessary skills and knowledge to include fathers. This lack of attention to fathers (particularly in the community service work education and curriculum) leaves frontline practice in a vulnerable state which is at risk of criticism from other disciplines[52,53]. If practitioners are aware of the factors that influence fathering[54] they are likely to be in a better position to identify some of the barriers or likely problems fathers face when they encounter a particular service or services[55]. Consequently, child and family welfare and other related services need to be responsive to fathers and mothers equally, with an emphasis on the caring relationships significant to children, regardless of whether this occurs in a heterosexual family or other forms of family types[56].

Involvement of fathers in community service practice

Community service practitioners have been involved with engaging with a diverse range of families for a very long time[57,58]. The very nature of the work involves a number of players, which can include the mother, child or children, the community service worker, foster carers, and others significant in the welfare of the child or children. Despite all the good practice that occurs with families, there still tends to be relatively poor engagement of men as fathers in community service with families. There are many reasons behind this gap in practice with fathers[59,60,61,62], however the most frequently identified within the literature include the perception that: men pose more of a domestic violence risk to women and children[63,64]; men can be intimidating to professionals[65]; men are hard to engage or reluctant users of services[66,67]; and that mothers are viewed as the protector and responsible for change even if the mother is the victim of abuse [68,69]. Additionally, recent research over the last decade has identified that community service practice with men as fathers can be difficult to locate, recruit and retain in practice [70,71,72,73,74,75].

A 2010 in-depth ethnographic study explored the methods of involving fathers in community service practice[76], and revealed a number of key themes which emerged about how professionals viewed the role of men as fathers in their practice. Firstly, community service practice generally focused only on the mothers. The term 'parent' was being used by professionals to describe the primary caretaker for bringing up children, but the term only applied in their practice to the mother, and often did not make reference to the father. Despite the existence of a father, mothers were the ones most often held responsible by family-service professionals for addressing and resolving problems in the family. In this study, the professionals generally found it difficult to locate fathers in their practice and overall were unable to see that involving fathers would lead to a more balanced and inclusive family support. Participants perceived involving fathers as complex, and that attempts from their own experiences with families had been met with little success. Yet inversely, practitioners did not regard including mothers in their practice as involving a similar level of complexity.

Secondly, the results suggested that professionals were more successful with involving fathers if the family was intact, that is, where both mother and father were present. Further, fathers were more likely to be included in a practitioner's practice if the mother had a good relationship with the father. A 'good relationship' according to the study participants consisted of stability within the couple relationship, a high degree of emotional support, and the absence of intimate partner violence or other undesirable behavioural issues such as alcohol or drug abuse. A father's inclusion in services would also be more beneficial to practitioners if the father was also physically available, which usually translated to residing in the same household. The more a father was physically unavailable or distant through work or other commitments, the less likely he would be included in case planning or clinical appointments for the family.

Lastly, practitioners viewed men as fathers more as risks than resources. The professionals in the study had limited understanding of diverse family types (sole parents, same gender, divorced, separated etc.) and often held beliefs that did not support the reality of contemporary family life. These findings are consistent with previous research that has highlighted a tendency among practitioners to avoid fathers irrespective if they are perceived to be risks or resources[77,78,79,80].

The results of this study suggest that practitioners need to identify which features of working with men as fathers can enable effective engagement to take place, while balancing workplace contextual factors that may enable or hinder a father's involvement[81]. Often services are comfortable recruiting fathers, but have trouble understanding how to maximise service impact[82]. There are also significant differences in fathers' willingness to engage with professionals. Fathers are a heterogeneous group and 'one size' does not fit all. A local approach needs to be part of an effective model of service delivery. Effective service delivery with fathers will only work if the fathers are genuinely involved and report that they feel connected to the service.

Effective service delivery: what have we learnt?

There are lots of different kinds of fathers. They may be in a two-parent family, in a stepfamily, be a full-time single parent, or have their children with them for some of the time. While parenting can be done by either parent, children have unique experiences with both their fathers and their mothers. Fathers sometimes only become active caregivers of their children by default or when necessity demands it; such as when the mother is unavailable or through change in employment status[83]. In addition, fathers may genuinely feel unsure about what is expected of them, which is due in part to the changing nature and role of fathers and mothers in today's society[84]. The major difference between men and women's experiences in managing these changes is that women more often articulate the changes they face as mothers, while fathers articulate less. This, ultimately, has an impact on their confidence and flexibility.

Family services need to focus on the family's individual needs to work out the best blend of roles played by the mother and father. Services can be responsive to the needs of fathers by asking them what they already do with their children, and what kinds of assistance they may require from staff and services. It is likely that men will be more suspicious about trusting a large organisation, as they are more likely to prefer a stronger connection to an individual practitioner to whom they respect. It is also important to begin working with those fathers already in contact with the service, as they may be able to assist in recruiting others. Where possible you should work in partnership with other services or practitioners who may be already engaged with fathers specifically.

Group work with fathers has also been shown to have a more positive impact than one-to-one counselling sessions or generic parenting programs such as Triple P on a father's well-being, particularly during times of stress and change in the family structure. Also, there is evidence that there is greater benefit in working in combination with couples than solely with fathers[85]. Yet, despite these developments, there is still evidence that we have a long way to go in making the rhetoric about engaging with men as fathers a reality.

CHAPTER 2:

ADVANTAGES OF INVOLVING FATHERS

Research indicates that fathers play a key role in raising active, vigorous, robust and thriving infants. Fitting with the research regarding risk and exploration attachment, infants seemed especially comfortable with, and attracted to, stimulation from the external environment. When practitioners exercise a greater involvement of fathers in their children's lives there are increased benefits for the children, mothers and men.

Fathers' attachment to their children

According to attachment theory a secure relationship is essential for a child's healthy development into adulthood[86]. Yet, studies investigating attachment and child development have focused almost exclusively on a child's relationships with their mother. Studies on attachment have shown that there are no differences between fathers' and mothers' potential abilities to develop an attachment to their children. It has been shown that fathers and mothers in a representative population are equally able to form a secure base for their children[87]. Due to an increased understanding of fathers' unique and crucial role in nurturing and guiding the child's development, many researchers now believe that fathers can be just as nurturing and sensitive with their babies as mothers, even if this is expressed differently[88]. Healthy child development relies on the roles played by both the mother and father respectively, whether they live together or apart. The early years of bonding and attachment[89] are crucial to the developing child's brain which sets the blueprint that impacts resilience and mental health outcomes for the rest of their lives[90].

In the few studies that do focus on fathering and child development there has been a shift in emphasis away from father involvement (presence/absence) to father sensitivity[91]. In doing so, research has identified that rather than quantity of time spent with a child, it is the quality of time spent with a child that is the most important[92]. For example, while a father may be at work or travelling for many hours each day, during the time they spend together the father might provide their child with a positive view of the world, emphasising that it is a safe place to live. As children grow and develop, fathers take on added roles of guiding their child's intellectual and social development.[93]

Due to social and cultural factors mothers and fathers interact with their children in different ways; fathers tend to play more physically and induce more excitement from their children than mothers do[94]. Early in a baby's life, the mother often holds a child for the purposes of care taking and nurturing, whereas a father holds the child for the purposes of playing[95]. When a father is 'just playing' they are nurturing the development of their children[96]. The fathers' interaction is often more active, stimulating, exciting, teasing, challenging and may even at times scare or arouse anxiety in the infant. These experiences serve an important purpose in children's lives, not just for their immediate care but also for their longer term development. In general terms the father's role can be described as one undertaken through play, challenge, risk taking, encouraging independence, and, later in development, helping the child to make the transition to the outside world[97].

Traditionally attachment theory has emphasised the significance of safety, comfort, and security as key factors in a child's development. It is now recognised that risk and exploration are equally important factors and are often undervalued. Figure 1, highlights that the child's experience of the play and challenge experiences with their father support the development of independence, risk taking, and the skills required for development throughout childhood into the larger social world[98]. A key focus in understanding this today is the experience of 'rough and tumble play'.

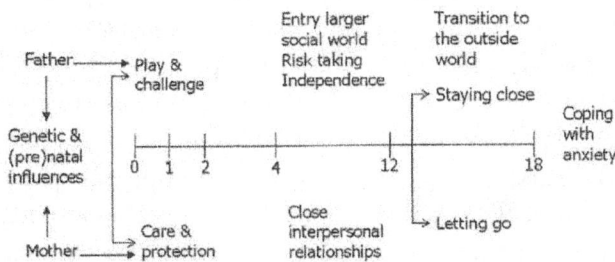

Figure 1: Different roles of fathers and mothers in their child's development (Bogels & Phares, 2008).

The special role of rough and tumble play

Rough and tumble play (RTP) is not equivalent to fighting between children. All mammals on the planet, especially the juveniles, have some form of rough and tumble play. In experiments, when rats are deprived of experiencing rough and tumble play they are much more anxious and likely to socially isolate[99]. In humans, playfulness is viewed as an activity that is fun or joyful while activating creativity or imagination[100].

> *One father said "I know he wants to wrestle when he gets that gleam in his eye. I chase him into the bedroom and he throws himself on our bed. I play the bulldozer. I put my head down and push and push until he falls off the bed onto the carpet. Other times we do world wrestling. I push him down on the bed, where I am going to slam him, but I do it really slowly, so that he has time to roll away before I crash down on the bed. There's lots of tickling too".* [101]

In humans, RTP is a physical activity that takes place in a playful context. It is characterised by:
- Wrestling, grappling, kicking and tumbling,
- Few rules,
- Being clearly distinguished from fighting,
- Enjoyment, not anger,
- Involves dominance swapping (different people take turns in 'winning'),
- Can involve the fathers teaching the skill of winning/losing with effort.

Children engage in various forms of RTP which addresses emotional regulation and social competence needs in children[102]. Because of its physical nature, RTP is often viewed by parents, caregivers and educators as an act of aggression rather than play. However, current research has highlighted that RTP is far more sophisticated than this perception and involves the development of socialisation amongst peers and emotional regulation within oneself toward others[103]. If RTP is not playful, it is aggression.

Fathers' RTP with their children therefore is important to promote an active, competitive, autonomous and curious attitude in children that is beneficial to the child's cognitive and social development. Recent research has identified that RTP was linked to Affective Social Competence (ASC). ASC is comprised of three integrated and dynamic components: sending affective messages, receiving affective messages, and experiencing affect[104].

ASC is an important contributor to children's optimal social and psychological functioning[105]. Additionally, RTP has been found to buffer early separation, stranger and social anxiety[106].

While the involvement of fathers has been associated with the rearing of boys, it is equally important for girls. Although boy's and girl's engage in different types of RTP, the physical and interactive form of play promotes emotional regulation and social competence in children. Fathers need to be more conscious of the important opportunity they have in the tendency to play with their children and actively develop more quality play experiences with their children. Furthermore, solo play time between fathers and their children can help the father develop their own parenting confidence without the mother being present. This is a key role that health professionals have in working with the family.

Does involving fathers improve support for the mothers?

Fathers have an important role to play in improving support for mothers. Eight-week-old infants can discriminate between their fathers and their mothers and respond in a differential way to their approach. In 1981, Yogman compared videotapes of comfortably seated infants' response to their mothers' approach and their fathers'[107]. In anticipation of their mothers' picking them up, babies settled in, slowed their heart and respiratory rates, and partially closed their eyes. When they expected their father to hold them, babies hunched up their shoulders, widened their eyes, and accelerated their heart and respiratory rates. Early research into fathering found that the more fathers participated in bathing, feeding, diapering, and other routines of physical care, the more socially responsive the babies were[108]. Statistics also show that one of the most significant indicators of breastfeeding rates at one and six-months is the *fathers' attitude towards breast feeding*. For this reason, and many more, it is vital that practitioners get dads involved in an increased capacity.

There have been many reported benefits for mothers when involving fathers in childbirth[109]:

- Women whose husbands were present and supportive during labour were less distressed[110,111].
- Labouring women benefit when they feel 'in control' of the birth process[112]. A key component of feeling in control is experiencing support from their partner during the birth.

- Support during delivery provided by a 'close support person' (who can be, and often is, the baby's father) creates a more positive childbirth experience for the mother, with a shorter duration of delivery and less pain experienced[113].
- When the support person (including father) knows a lot about pain control options during labour, women have shorter labours and are less likely to have epidurals[114].
- When women are more supported during childbirth, they develop more positive attitudes to motherhood[115].

A home visit reflection

"Our early childhood nurse was very supportive. When she did the first visit after the birth of our child, she engaged with both my wife and I in how we can care for our son. After she discussed breast feeding with the mum, she turned to me and asked me to stand up and move to the other side of the room. She asked me to look at the angle of how my son was positioned on my wife's lap. She encouraged me to remember this, as it will be useful feedback if my son was not connecting with the breast and getting distressed. That weekend, that is what happened. My son was distressed; my wife was exhausted and was getting upset. I was able to stand back and encourage her to lift the head a bit more. It worked, and my son attached".

In difficult situations, it is crucial to remind fathers to encourage the mothers to maintain breastfeeding and seek professional support.

Men need education about labour and childbirth processes so that they are aware of what to expect when they accompany their partners for childbirth. This understanding will enable them to better support their partners emotionally throughout the birthing process[116]. Different ways that practitioners can assist fathers in supporting their partner include[117]:

- In childbirth classes, divide the mothers and support people into separate small group discussions for a short time so they can both more openly discuss the challenges of childbirth that they each experience.
- Provide expectant father classes that cater for their information needs with easy-to-read handouts and materials relevant for them as the support person.
- Use practical examples of how men can be supportive. It is important

to provide active examples for how they can support their partner through the birth process.

- Encourage the reflection and involvement of fathers in childbirth classes. Fathers who have been prepared well to participate productively in the labour process tend to be more active participants, and their partners' birth-experiences tend to be better.

- Use the personal testimony of a mother and father who recently had a child to talk to the next class about their reflections and experiences.

- Recognise the psychological boost the fathers can provide as a support person. Medical professionals greatly underestimate the psychological boost fathers give to their partners during delivery – as well as the practical support the men provide during labour, and afterwards.

Involving fathers to support mothers with post-natal depression

When mothers have post-natal depression, the father's functioning as a support person is critical as the women often receive more support from their partner than from any other individual, including medical staff[118]. Some studies have shown that:

- A Canadian randomised control study involving partners in support programs for the mothers with postnatal depression found that when the women's partner participated in 4 out of 7 psycho-educational visits, the women displayed a significant decrease in depressive symptoms and other psychiatric conditions[119]. When only the women (and not their partner) received the intervention the general health of the depressed women's partners deteriorated. This effect was not found where the men were included in the intervention[120].

- A shorter length of hospital stay among women with pre/postpartum psychiatric disorders is strongly and positively correlated with supportiveness by their (male) partners. However, only 30% of these men are categorized by the researchers as supportive[121].

- A brief and inexpensive US intervention (one prenatal session, in separate gender groups focusing on psychosocial issues related to becoming first-time parents) was associated with reduced distress in mothers at six-weeks postpartum[122].

- Fathers, as well as the mothers, can experience physical and/or emotional disturbances after the birth of children[123]. These may include feelings of sadness, anxiety, irritability, poor concentration, changes to appetite, sleeping difficulties, and increased intake of alcohol or drugs. These feelings may be related to life changes, personal or relationship issues, fears or concerns either parent may have.

Professionals can encourage both the mother and father to:

- Work as a team to tackle this challenge in their life.
- Allow family and friends to support and help.
- Learn about post-partum depression and ways they can support each other.
- Share their thoughts and feelings with each other.
- Focus on their shared dreams for their child and family
- Spend time engaging in pleasant activities as a family.
- Create an environment that allows each of them to engage in positive interaction with their baby.
- Create an environment that allows each of them to have some time for themselves.
- Maintain regular contact with family and friends.
- Nurture each other.
- Go for a walk and eat nutritious meals.
- Take time out to rest.
- Join a group where they can have contact with other parents.
- Consult their local doctor, therapist/counsellor or nurse and develop supportive networks.

Making the most of parental leave opportunities

Even though the Commonwealth Government provides legislation that supports men having parental leave (2 weeks of paid leave at the minimum wage), many men still cannot utilise this opportunity as they are casual practitioners, self-employed or work in a context where employers are less supportive. Kaufman[124] interviewed a small group of United Kingdom couples and identified that men may not take parental leave due to financial concerns, gendered expectations, perceived workplace resistance, and lack of flexibility in available leave options.

Where possible, parental leave should be encouraged by health professionals as it can have significant consequences for the whole family. Parental leave supports parents to[125]:

- Develop more stable couple relationships;

- Maintain higher levels of contact with children, should mothers and fathers subsequently separate;
- Adopt healthier lifestyle (by the father) and reduced mortality risk. There is a decreased risk of "all-cause mortality" indicators amongst men who take between 30 and 135 days of parental leave[126];
- Increase in the father's role in caretaking throughout the child's life; and,
- Reduce the likelihood of mothers 'smoking, become depressed, and increase likelihood of breastfeeding.

Benefits for children's development

Due to the ethical challenges of conducting a study that measures children's outcomes, most studies have looked at improvements in fathers' skills or father-and-child interactions as 'proxies' for benefits to children[127].Programs involving fathers have observed the following benefits to children[128]:

- Improved social competence,
- Reduced anxiety,
- Children with higher self-esteem,
- Better health outcomes and reduction in obesity,
- Increased cognitive benefits, and
- Healthier relationships with peers.

Current research indicates that supportive, positive play between fathers and their young children has also been associated with enhanced cognitive development and reduced developmental delays among disadvantaged children[129]. These effects are also maintained throughout childhood and adolescence. Community service and health programs would transform their service provision if they took this research seriously. The starting point is recognising the significant advantages to supporting strong-father-child ties.

Sons and dads

Boys who have engaged, supportive fathers[130]:

- Do better academically and achieve more financially rewarding employment.
- Have higher self-esteem throughout adolescence and their entire lives.
- Are less likely to be aggressive to other children or adults or get hurt themselves.

- Go on to form loving relationships with their partners.
- Have better coping mechanisms to help them get through the stresses of modern life.

Daughters and dads

Evidence from a systematic review of 18 studies, has indicated that father engagement positively affects social, behavioural[131], psychological and cognitive outcomes[132] of children. More specifically, high levels of father involvement have been linked to girls who have connected, loving relationships with their father (or a male role model who is close to them)[133].

Importance of involving separated fathers

A well designed 2009 longitudinal study of a group US of adolescents explored what impact closeness to their father had on their life[134]. It controlled for the difference in age and how adolescents may respond differently to either the mother or father. It found that:

1. Adolescents who are close to their non-resident fathers report higher self-esteem, less delinquency, and fewer depressive symptoms than adolescents who live with a father with whom they are not close.
2. There was no difference between the two groups with respect to school grades, being involved in violent activities or substance use.
3. Not being close to a resident father is associated with lower self-esteem compared to having a non-resident father who is not close.
4. Adolescents do best of all when they have close ties to resident fathers. A central conclusion of this study is that it is important to consider the quality of father–child relations among those who have a resident father when assessing the impact of non-resident fathers on their children.
5. Closeness to fathers reduces violence similarly in resident-father families and non-resident-father families.

In summary, the evidence from cross-sectional and longitudinal research into infancy, childhood, and adolescence suggests that the father has an important and unique role in child development. In general terms, the father's role can be described as one which is undertaken through play, challenge, risk-taking, encouraging independence and in later development by helping the child make the transition to the outside world[135]. It is therefore important to encourage fathers to develop strong attachments with their children, as it will benefit not only the child but also the father, their relationship and society in general.

Chapter 3:
Valuing fathering –
A non-deficit approach

When working with men, professionals often view fathering from a deficit perspective[136]. The deficit perspective assumes that men are largely uninvolved and uninterested in the lives of their children and unwilling to change. This assumption is supported by cultural narratives of separated fathers who are uninterested in being involved with their children and do not support their children financially. Some people are suspicious of young men caring for young children and assume that fathers are incapable of adequately caring for the basic needs of young children. In the community services sector, practitioners may view men to be inadequate when it comes to parenting due to the special needs of the families with whom they work and the impact of domestic violence.

How deficit perspectives are expressed

Deficit assumptions are expressed in a variety of contexts[137]. They include assumptions of the abusing father, the 'emotionally challenged' father fathers under involvement in household activities, and the fathers have little interest in professional feedback about their children.

The 'abusing' father

Russell et al (1999)[138] identified that 48% of community welfare professionals believe that up to 24% of fathers physically abuse their children and 31% of professionals believed that 24% of fathers sexually abused their children. These figures are higher than the national statistics on child abuse and neglect or domestic violence and these assumptions may influence how caseworkers and counsellors develop a trusting relationship with most fathers. Instead it is important to work from a position of ethical interest that builds on the man's aspiration to be a better father.

The 'emotionally challenged' father

There are a range of labels used to describe fathers, both formally and informally, that include: incompetent, unaware, fear of intimacy, emotionally constricted, emotionally constipated and the like. Professionals are divided on whether these emotionally challenged fathers need a strong adult male mentor or a skilled and patient therapist who can guide them through their dangerous inner journeys to healthy responsible manhood. However, there is common agreement that most men are emotionally and relationally deficient and need to be changed.

Fathers under involvement in household activities

According to the Household, Income and Labour Dynamics in Australia (HILDA) Survey men's engagement in housework has increased over time, from 12.4 hours per week in 2002 to 13.3 hours in 2016[139]. This contrasts with the 20.4 hours per week, on average, that women, spent on household chores each week in 2016. This statistic is regrettable, and supports the idea that men are uninvolved, selfishly resisting change and greater involvement with the brunt of household cleaning and child rearing done by women. Yet, recent results from the Multinational Time Use Study suggests that while women still do the majority of household work, men continue to spend more time in paid employment[140]. The amount of total work (paid and unpaid work) done is much the same for men and women[141].

Fathers have little interest in professional feedback about their children

When health/community welfare professionals provide feedback to families regarding issues that affect their children, they often favour delivering this information to the mother. This assumption reinforces other beliefs that fathers are deficient in their interest in their knowledge concerning the basic health needs of their children.

There are many reasons that fathers play a secondary role in health/ community welfare relationships. Most significantly, appointment times are during the day when it is difficult for men or women who work in full-time employment to have time off. However, men can question or be wary of involvement with external community welfare agencies. Many men often have a strong suspicion about people who influence their family life. Their experience in receiving support from others is much more limited compared to that of many women. A key aspect of working with men during initial engagement is the importance of reducing the level of suspicion by creating relevance, being a believer in the significant role they play and by using honest/ direct communication. Apart from the insights of family members, many men have little trust and question the relevance of new ideas about the relationships in their life.

From boyhood, competitiveness is nurtured that teaches young men that they should not 'be walked over by other people'. This process continues as the child grows into a man, entrenching values of independence and autonomy. For many men, a suggestion that they need to change what they are thinking or doing is met by a high degree of resistance. Especially when a suggestion contains a deficit assumption like 'men should show more of their feelings.' This assumption is that something needs to be fixed; the father must learn to act differently. Due to this, professionals need to work hard at the pre-engagement stage when working with fathers to find an alternative way to dealing with the defensiveness (this will be discussed further in this chapter).

All these assumptions highlight the deficiencies of men at the expense of acknowledging that the basic motivational force for many men is a deep love for their family and the desire to be a good dad. While the deficit assumption may adequately describe the behaviour of many dads, it lacks the potential for engaging men and creating life change. Deficit assumptions create little change in fathers because[142]:

- They have little recognition of growth and development.
- They misconstrue the motives, feelings, attitudes, and hopes of most fathers.
- They create barriers to change rather than its promotion.
- They have a narrow standard of good parenting.
- The following case study highlights how deficit assumptions either encourage men to give up or to try twice as hard.

Case Study

George is 43 years old and his two-year-old daughter is currently in foster care. He ceased his heroin use several years previously and was currently attending an intensive fathering program (18-months). Sally, the mother of the child, lives with a new boyfriend who is violent towards Sally. When George joined the Fathers Group, he was angry, resentful, and very distrustful of the system. Primarily, he wanted his daughter to be safe, and since living currently with the mother would not ensure her safety, he sought to be the primary caregiver. He was resentful that the child protection agency would not take seriously his commitment to be the resident father.

Early in the group, it became apparent that George had very good insight into the emotional and developmental needs of his daughter. However, throughout his life he had always been under appreciated by key people in his life. The group provided an environment to validate the important role he wanted to play as a father, and to gain recognition and support. The group leader's support gave George one of the few times in his life that he had experienced someone supporting him. The group learnt about how George had ceased his poly-drug use once he became a father (he referred to the birth of his daughter as a wake-up call). During the course of the group, he also ceased all alcohol use and played a very important support role in the group for other members. By the time George went to court, the independent clinical psychologist stated that in 25 years of practice he had never see anyone else make such a change to their life. George's love for his daughter provided the basic motivation to sustain this significant life change.

An alternative perspective of fathering

Fathering is seen in a different light when alternative assumptions are adopted. Strengths based practice has a high level of efficacy in working with women, children, young people, those with disabilities and culturally diverse communities[143]. The non-deficit perspective (also known as a strengths-based perspective) recognises that most fathers want their role to be different from how they were fathered, and that good fathering is something which is necessary to their own well-being and fundamental life motivation. It also suggests that a father's care for his children is a 'central feature of his life's work and you would expect him to strive for competence in this arena'[144]. Yet, using strengths-based approaches does not mean practitioners need to condone violence or inappropriate behaviours. Strengths-based approaches allows those more difficult conversations to happen as practitioners talk more directly about any behaviours that threaten their relationship and family. Effective fathering programs validate different aspects of what the men are already doing well. It is then, that greater freedom is generated to explore the barriers that prevent men from achieving what they desire.

Many men identify fathering as something which is active, challenging, creative, irreplaceable, hard work and a central part of their life. The centrality of positive child relationships is often reported regardless of the state of other family relationships (e.g. relationship/or lack thereof with the child's mother). The cornerstone of understanding fathering is through the generative experience, where men re-evaluate their life and work towards the care and protection of their children throughout their whole lifetime.

Case Study

Peter is a father in an intact relationship, where he has two children. Peter commenced attending the fathers program after his first child died as a toddler from a respiratory problem. He had loved his daughter so much; he was heartbroken. He and his partner attended only one session of grief counselling. Throughout the years following his child's death the stress of fathering and fear for the safety of his other children through their early life took its toll on his relationship with his wife. This was also exacerbated by his imminent retrenchment from work. By being in the program, Peter was able to talk for the first time around his grief for his first child. He was also able to remove much of the pressure that had been building inside of him. Over six months, Peter successfully moved back home and continued to play the vital role in the family that he had played previously.

Developing a non-deficit perspective of fathering

The non-deficit perspective views fathers, until proven otherwise, as having a basic motivation for the best care and protection of their children. Hawkins and Dollahite argue that most fathers value moral, productive, mature and loving relationships[145]. These responsibilities and capabilities represent 'essential things that fathers *should do*, *want to do*, *can do* and *actually do* for their children. We believe that the needs of children call fathers to use their fathering capabilities to meet those needs'[146]. This perspective identifies that fathers can choose (in certain constraints and contexts) to live these values.

The non-deficit perspective recognises that fathers have the desire and the ability to:

- Commit -The physical and ongoing support that a father provides and his awareness and involvement with the child throughout their lifetime.
- Choose - The capacity to make day to day decisions for their children that meet the child's needs.
- Care - The ability to attend to the important transitions in a child's life and provide the optimal conditions that maximise their growth.
- Change - The ability to adapt as children grow older and the father matures in his relationship with the children.
- Create - The creation of resources for material comfort and the resolution of problems that allow opportunities for the development of emotional well-being.
- Connect - The ability to form lasting and healthy attachments with their children. These attachments will change over time to meet the child's evolving needs.
- Communicate - The capacity to relate with children by sharing meaningfully with them, both verbally and non-verbally.

Further, men are more likely to engage and access community agencies when they feel safe and valued. This is done using non-deficit approaches that recognise that families and their children are a central motivation in most fathers' lives. Rather than men feeling that they need to be fixed or changed, a practitioner can work beside the father to create a mutual change process.

Non-deficit techniques to engage fathers

There are a range of strategies that can be used to implement the non-deficit perspective.

Deepen the father's motivation to develop a close relationship with his child.

Amongst the many and varied descriptions of masculinity, the non-deficit perspective identifies that in many men, their relationship with their children is a very significant connection. As previously noted, this connection can be viewed as 'the quiet place within' that most men talk about least. It is a personal space that men rarely share. Many men only start talking about the importance of their family relationships after a relationship crisis such as family separation has occurred.

Recently, men are becoming more vocal about the importance of their connection with their family, particularly their children. What is occurring is a quiet men's revolution. This men's revolution is not as vocal as the women's movement, but it is noticed as men talk about achieving a better balance between work and family demands. The change is seen by how men behave differently as they walk hand-in-hand with their children and proudly push the pram. Some men identify the reason for attend a fathering program, is because they want to father their children differently to how they were fathered. The birth of a child is now a 'wake-up call' for many men and an opportunity for them to review the choices they make in life and provides the motivation to develop stronger relationships. It is also demonstrated through the loss of identity after family separation occurs, especially in relation to their involvement with their children.

The shadowy side of men's behaviour still exists. It is captured in the horrifying and non-changing national family violence statistics. It is in this context that many men and family relationship services operate. The challenge for programs is to engage men in working with this "quiet space". The non-deficit perspective does not condone inappropriate male behaviours but harnesses the positive motivations that makes change a reality. Once this quiet space is entered into and men are engaged in accessing men and family relationship programs, the skills used by practitioners in working with women can be applied to working with men.

While significant achievements have occurred in working with men[147] the challenge is still enormous. The 2008 National Male Health Policy[148] identified that men have major health problems. They have high rates of depression, suicide, violence, drug and alcohol use and fatal motor vehicle accidents. It recognises that there is still a strong belief that men do not ask for help but fix themselves. Promotion of fathering programs still needs improvement as many men view the word 'counselling' as a punitive response for workplace misdemeanours. It is still common for men to remark 'I never thought such services for men existed' when they first contact a fathering program. This responsiveness to crisis rather than prevention is also mirrored in how men visit their doctor less than women and only seek help only after a crisis has occurred when some part of their everyday functioning has been reduced.

The inflexibility of Australian workplaces (at the shop, factory or self-employment level) and the widespread existence of family violence are still significant issues that confront programs as men usually access programs only when a crisis occurs. A variety of public awareness campaigns have been useful in promoting a responsive environment that encourages the proactive view that it is okay for men to seek help before the crisis occurs.

Case Study

Sam is an 18-year-old young dad who lived in detention centres and had been involved with the police since the age of twelve. At the birth of his first son, he decided to stop stealing cars and doing home robberies. The birth of his child had a profound effect on him. However, his troubled childhood and pent up anger, negatively affected his partner and himself. A child welfare agency ended up removing the baby. Throughout the past six-months, Sam has been committed to developing new ways of dealing with old situations. At present he is walking away when tensions are high and recognises the impact that his violence has had on his child. Through ceasing to use marijuana, he is discovering a greater motivation for creating stability in his life and is arguing less with his partner. Instead of bottling everything up inside, he sits down and talks problems through. Sam still has many things to learn, but one thing is sure. His commitment to his child has been a fundamental motivation for many lifestyle changes.

Practice active outreach on an individual level.

It is vital to use a range of promotional strategies for engaging fathers. While it is important to use local newspapers to promote positive aspects of fathering, it primarily informs the wider community and extended family members about available programs. Men are generally cautious and suspicious of fliers promoting programs and activities. They are more likely to respond to recommendations and prompts from trusted family members. It is important to encourage other professionals in your area to speak directly to fathers they know about forthcoming group activities.

It is important to have a direct face-to face or telephone discussion as part of every intake process. During this initial discussion, practitioners need to work to relieve father's suspicions and create a strong connection between the fathers' motivation and the role of the program in supporting them. Without strong relationships being established early on, fathers will have a limited engagement with a service.

Case study

> *Dennis was very tentative about coming to the group. In the end he was encouraged to attend the first session and to tell the group leader their honest opinion about if the group was interesting or boring. Dennis is still attending the group nine months later. He reflected, 'I thought it would be just a lecture' but it was very different than he expected.*

Listen carefully to the unique stories, needs and strengths of fathers.

Stories can be a familiar and safe way of communicating with men. They provide a context where respect and a deeper focus on mutual concerns are developed. Since fathers do not often use opportunities to tell other men significant stories about their family life, it generates a lot of interest and curiosity to hear other men talking about their life. The art of working with stories can trigger the movement from the known to the unknown. This is generated through critical questioning that reviews a story in a different shape and form.

The creative use of strategic questioning[149] can easily be applied to the context of working with fathers. *Strategic questioning creates new information and uncovers deep desires of the heart rather than communicating information already known.* The power of this questioning framework lies in the obser-vation questions near the beginning of the process. Observation questions like, 'what have you already learned about XXXX?; where did you learn that from?, place the client in a position of power, agency and strength. They assess the validity of the information/situation that is impacting on their life. Also, the personal inventory and support questions near the end are a powerful way to recognise that change does not happen in a vacuum; it needs to be supported by others. It is conversational - describing ideas and experiences in an informal way. It challenges and extends - through the reflection of other stories or examining the same story in a different way. It works from a place of equality where no insight is necessarily better than another.

Case Study

Bob is a very loud and brash person. Besides struggling through his second separation, and a court case regarding his behaviour at the last break-up, he also experiences depression. Silence is difficult for Bob, so he fills the time with much of his own talk. The challenge for Bob is to slow down and hear what other people are saying. This is immensely difficult, but Bob's involvement in the father's program has been vital as he has applied this learning to his family relationships.

Acknowledge some of the positive characteristics (strengths) that men bring to parenting.

Men parent in different ways to women. A male way of parenting is often very active and involves being out and about in the world. When men are primary caregivers of young children, they often identify childcare as their main task. Because of this, they may spend less time around the home and are more mobile going on excursions, trips to the parks and walking with children. Their social identity as a father is not in connection to the house or completion of household tasks.

Many fathers are focused on the big picture issues in life. Men tend to focus more on issues affecting lifelong role of caring and protecting their children. They can spend more time in forward planning and preparing for forthcoming years. This may mean that they will need some coaching in how to deal with immediate issues. However, the father's focus on their children is often a central motivation in their life.

For example, families that have a child with a special needs experience many challenges and stresses. Many men cope with this situation the best they can by working long hours, thereby ensuring the family has adequate finances. Besides their partner, men with a disabled child often have few people to talk with regarding the impact of the special needs. When a professional uses deficit assumption to work with the father, they focus on the man's isolation, the working of long hours and his lack of communication. Alternatively, the non-deficit perspective would focus on valuing the underlying motivation the father experiences, namely, the care and protection of their children and family. This allows a much richer discussion and more opportunities to discuss the impact of the decisions the men are making.

Respect the issues that women have worked hard to change

Women have worked very hard to receive the recognition that they deserve. Not only are many women in full time employment but they still play the primary roles for parenting and maintaining the household. To ensure appropriate changes occur for both parents, old stereotypes have been let go and new non-deficit images of competence and confidence have been adopted. It is important that programs do not focus on men's rights or women's rights, but what is in the best interest of the children. It is in this context that children, mothers and fathers can prosper mutually.

Research has identified teamwork parenting as an important strategy to engage fathers. In 2009, Cowan[150] conducted a randomized control evaluation of an intervention to increase fathers' engagement. Participants were randomly assigned to either a 16-week group for fathers, a 16-week group for couples, or a 1-time informational meeting. Results from an 18-month follow-up demonstrated that both the longer interventions produced superior effects for fathers' engagement with their children, couple relationship quality, and children's behaviour as compared to the lower dose condition. However, only the parents from the couples' groups showed significant declines in parenting stress. The inclusion of both parents in any parenting interventions is very important. It is important to emphasize that practitioners need to be cautious in working with couples if domestic violence is occurring. Best practice wisdom indicates that it is essential to provide a range of choices for engaging fathers that include working individually with both parents, providing groups that target the parents as a couple and the provision of fathers' groups.

Chapter 4:

Principles for effective practice with fathers

Having an involved father has obvious benefits to children. Recent media coverage on fathers identify the clear benefits of fathers being involved in a child's life, particularly in the early stages of development, by providing love, support, and comfort[151]. We can probably also agree that fathers are important because they help to teach children values and lessons in solving life's challenges and problems. Fathers also serve as role models in their child's life, which can affect how well their children relate to peers and adults outside the home[152].

In order to support involved fathering, practitioners must first acknowledge some key assumptions on father inclusion. These are:
- That most fathers want to be effective parents.
- Parenting experience for either mother or father is a highly complex and challenging role.
- By including fathers it conveys a message that we have positive expectations of them and they in turn respond by being involved and aspire to being the best fathers they can be.
- Fathers will require support from the wider environment, external to the family[153].

Furthermore, some researchers have even argued that fathering and fatherhood is greatly influenced by family and community factors more than the mother[154]. Awareness of your own interactions with fathers is the first step towards supporting involved fathering. The following questions are meant to be a guide to help to your own self-assessment as a practitioner on interactions with fathers:
- How do you acknowledge the presence of a father on your first interaction?

- Do you include fathers in the conversation when both caregivers are present?
- What is your body language saying that indicates inclusion?
- Do you have eye contact with the father or is it directed at the mother/ other caregiver?
- Do you include fathers in discussions about their children or respond to father's questions about their child?
- What are your own beliefs about fathers and their ability to take on child care tasks?

Whilst most agencies and services will have father inclusiveness some-where in their policy and procedures or strategic planning, the most effec-tive method of supporting fathers begins with the practitioner. For some practitioners they may already be achieving the goal of involving fathers, for others, more reflection is required. It does not matter where you are on this continuum, what matters is that you have taken the time to do some reflection and taken steps to improve or fine tune your practice with fathers. This process can be initiated by following 8 basic principles for working effectively with fathers.

1. Importance of perceived equality

When there is a significant power difference between the service providers and the father, men will be more cautious and wary of engagement. There-fore, programs that have a high level of client participation are more effec-tive in engaging fathers. This emphasis on equality is reflected in the notion of 'mateship' and has been a defining feature of male culture since the settlement of Australia[155] and pre-existed in Indigenous Australia. This is important, as fathers often feel they have little control or influence in many aspects of their lives.

2. Existence of 'window periods' where men access support

For some fathers experiencing problems in their lives, there is the potential for a 'window period' during which they are more likely to access services for assistance. These window periods reflect life crises that may occur where their life is no longer working as expected, e.g. the birth of the first child, family separation, retirement, and having a child with special needs etc. If they experience high levels of frustration and are unable to access services because of long waiting lists or complicated referral procedures, they are likely to give up trying and find other solutions to deal with their problems. These solutions frequently include ignoring the problem or reacting in more aggressive ways because of their pent-up feelings.

Some organisations have attempted to make intake procedures and personal information forms more user-friendly as men have a higher level of frustration when they do not understand those processes. The comparatively higher levels of male illiteracy can be accommodated by using more visual and experiential ways for learning rather than the sole use of text.

3. The need for fathering services to be distinguished from general parenting services

Programs for men need to have a strong branding about the services being male-focused or for fathers. Unless the word *fathers* or *men* are used in the program title, men assume that the program is not relevant to them. There was a significant increase in men accessing parenting when they used specific fliers that used the word 'dads' and indicated the relevance of the program to fathers. Further, when school-based programs used an invitation to attend a special event that is written and coloured in by their child, fathers attended in very large numbers.

4. The value of personal recommendation about services

In the initial stages of operation many father's programs experience low numbers of referrals and participants. In this start-up period, professionals need to persevere when the initial response by men to a program is not as high as anticipated. Low client numbers in male focused programs are often interpreted as an indicator of male disinterest, although this phenomenon frequently occurs across community programs.

Many fathers will attend programs because of the recommendation of friends, 'mates' or family members. It is only after a period that programs develop a routine and consistency in service provision. This may include ongoing support groups, regular educational groups or even 1-day workshops that are run every 6-months. It is the consistency over a long period, which builds a program's reputation as being effective and worthwhile.

One of the strongest forms of marketing occurs when someone whom a man trusts recommends they access a program. This referral is more effective when the client is given a direct telephone number and a specific name of a contact person at the service. Further, fathers may stop seeking help when they feel frustrated by their difficulties in contacting someone or accessing support. Services should focus on providing prompt and inclusive responses in-person or via telephone. Additionally, it is useful for programs to obtain support from significant local employers so they can use corporate logos to support their promotion of fathering messages and events.

5. The importance of flexible service delivery

Fathers' services need to provide a range of group programs that offer choice. Men have a higher level of commitment when they can choose their level of involvement. Some of those choices include men accessing:
- intensive fathers' groups and emotional support groups where participants attend for six to fifteen months (mid-week evening);
- educational groups that have a duration of six to eight weeks (mid-week evening);
- information based, one-day workshops delivered on the weekend;
- father/child playgroups provided midweek or on the weekend;
- counselling; and
- telephone support.

Even if your program provides only playgroups, when you talk with a new prospective male client, suggest a range of options i.e. post out some info, talk again later or come along to the next playgroup.

Since 2000, a diverse range of local initiatives have been trialled across Australia that respond to father's needs[156]. Avoiding the "one-size fits all" approach to service delivery, programs for fathers have been used across various communities can include:
- Afternoon/evening programs for fathers and their children held in primary schools that involve activities and a shared meal.
- Support groups for separated fathers on Sunday evenings after contact with their children finishes.
- Psychoeducational fathering groups or fathering after separation or domestic violence programs.

- Specialised programs for Indigenous and culturally and linguistically diverse men.
- The range of programs (one-off workshops or psychoeducational groups) and information booklets that have been developed by the Commonwealth Government's Child Support Agency.
- Counselling and emotional support groups – where men explore a range of experiences.
- Individual counselling services provided out of normal working hours.
- Programs delivered through the workplace.
- Programs accessed by new fathers before they leave the hospital with their first baby
- Task groups and the development of Men's Sheds where a range of activities are provided.
- Camp/adventure programs for fathers or for men and their children.
- Music festivals that promote messages of fathering and positive messages about masculinity.
- 'Pit-stop' men's health check-up evenings provided in regional Club facilities throughout regional areas of Australia.
- Family farm gatherings in rural communities where 6-7 families meet to discuss issues affecting drought affected communities.
- Telephone group counselling sessions.
- Telephone counselling and support programs for individuals.

Fathers approach community organisations to meet their specific and immediate needs. When agencies provide several of the above programs, they are more likely to cater for the diverse range of men's needs. Fathers often decide if a community program is relevant to their needs in the first few minutes of initial contact, when they are either talking on the telephone or walking in the front entrance of an agency.

Men are easily frustrated by bureaucracy, especially when they see themselves as part of an impersonal system. Men value learning from peers where the emphasis is on equality rather than power-based relationships. They are more likely to place a greater importance on self-care (and less likely to believe that they are indestructible) when they reflect on their lifelong responsibilities to other significant people in their life.

6. Client involvement in program development

It is important for service providers to involve their male clients in shaping and determining the most effective strategies to achieve program outcomes.

When services are developing new programs or groups for fathers it is vital to establish local reference groups that involve this target group. These reference groups can provide important feedback about program direction, marketing, and ambassadors who can personally recommend the program to other fathers.

Men who receive valuable support from a community program may develop a strong interest in volunteering and supporting the program's further development. This energy is a tremendous resource. When combined with adequate training and mentoring, this energy can result in positive outcomes for both the fathers and the service. New generations of men are emerging who have the experience to engage and support fathers who are not accessing other parenting programs.

7. Solution-focused approach

Men often prefer solution-focused activities rather than just talking about their problems[157]. The focus is not on feelings but improved relationships with significant people in the men's lives. A key factor in the use of solution-focused frameworks is the adoption of a non-deficit approach to working with men that searches for solutions that are oriented around the importance of the relationship between men and their children.

8. Local area coordination

A defining feature to improve father engagement at a regional level is the development of practice support networks. Due to the low number of men employed in community welfare/health programs, practitioner isolation is a key in fathering programs. Using the network to promote and support practice is essential. The network meetings have provided opportunities for sharing information and allowed for the exploration of issues in greater depth.

Four key areas for effective service delivery with fathers

The remainder of this chapter discusses four key areas for effective delivery practice with fathers and how organisations can improve engagement and program provision to fathers. These areas include the environment, language, initial contact and marketing, and service provision. A checklist concludes the chapter that can be completed to assess a program's strengths and weaknesses when working with fathers.

1. The environment

When a father makes initial contact with a program their level of trust will be influenced by the immediate environment and openness of staff towards them. Fathers may enter new family services with suspicion about what will be expected of them and rely on visual cues to relax. Some environmental factors that organisations can use to increase engagement are:

  i.   Use positive images of men in posters and having suitable reading material in the waiting rooms that may interest men, which provide an easy read and positive reflection on fathering. Display photographs of events that especially feature images of men and children.

  ii. When possible, employ male staff to work directly with male and female clients.

  iii. Train and support all your practitioners (regardless of their gender) to work directly and confidently with fathers on their caseload. This is instead of siloing, where male clients are only seen by the male staff member.

  iv. Use premises that are easily accessible, with car parking space or access to public transport. In unfamiliar situations, everyone, including men, often tolerate a low level of frustration and may give up accessing a program if it seems too hard.

  v.   Focus on deeper engagement of male clients using initial telephone contact. Fathers often use the telephone as the first point of contact to reach out for support. They may telephone many agencies to locate an organisation that will be helpful to them. This can result in confusion when practitioners return telephone calls, as the potential client may not immediately remember the specific organisation that they had called.

  vi. When referring fathers to another service, provide them with the specific name of someone to contact and what makes the referral relevant to their situation rather than only providing a generic number and program name. When the referral is more relationship rich, fathers may be more likely to follow through with the connection.

  vii. Provide services outside normal working hours. Many fathers find it difficult to access community programs while working part time or full time. It is still easier for male clients to access programs when they are offered on weekends or in the evenings.

viii. Ensure that large power differences do not exist between practitioners and the clients. When culturally appropriate, encourage staff to use the first name of the father rather than more formal greetings like 'Mr Jones…'.

ix. When holding occasional workshops, use venues where men normally gather (e.g., sporting venues or events and specific workplaces). These spaces provide opportunities for promoting programs and recruiting fathers. Men from specific cultural groups may more likely attend an event at a local religious institution rather than a sporting venue[158].

x. In schools, early childhood centres or childcare centres, ask the children to write or colour-in an invitation for their father to attend a special event at the centre. Then ask them to give it to their dad. If the child does not have a father, encourage them to give to another important male in their life e.g. uncle or grandfather or coach.

xi. Sometimes, men are more likely to attend a child and family service if they are encouraged to do so by their partners. Similarly, a partner who discourages his involvement may reduce a man's willingness to engage with a service.

2. Language

Language has a significant influence on the successful engagement of many fathers. If the language used by the practitioner is deficit based, it will increase the man's level of suspicion and they are less likely to access the program. Some of the deficit-based assumptions[159] position men as abusers, emotionally challenged, under involved in household activities and as having little interest in professional feedback about their children. When working with men effective language primarily involves three key components as illustrated in Figure 2. The use of the following three skills occurs wholly within the workplace safety policy.

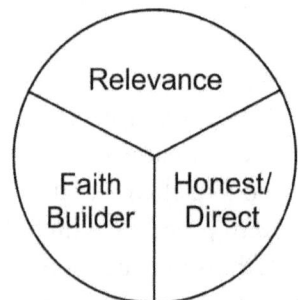

Workplace Safety

Relevance

Faith Builder

Honest/ Direct

The three key components[160] for developing father-friendly language are:

- **Relevant** – the discussion needs to be relevant to the client's immediate needs and situation.
- **Faith building** – the practitioner needs to convey the belief that the male client can commit, choose, care, change, create, connect and communicate.
- **Honest/direct** – Most male clients respect people who honestly and respectfully discuss with them the important issues that affect their life.

Important communication strategies that increase engagement with men include:

i. Remember that body language is powerful. Develop strong and comfortable body language around male clients regardless of any height or size differences. Men quickly tune into how comfortable other people are around them and this will influence their level of respect. The simple act of shaking hands, for many men, can symbolise a higher level of respect and mutual connection. In different cultural groups and age brackets, a 'high five' (if the person is well known) will achieve the same effect or standing a suitable distance apart and confidently introducing yourself may be appropriate.

ii. Use non-deficit language to demonstrate a respect for the importance of family relationships in men's lives and for those basic human values which are important to them.

iii. Allow time for male clients to reflect on a discussion after you have been honest and direct with them. Men can become frustrated and need an opportunity to vent their feelings and time to consider the importance of what has been said. However, no form of intimidation or threat of violence or aggression is acceptable. Sometimes offering an idea as a suggestion and allowing them time to reflect is far better than saying this is what they need to do.

iv. Be comfortable with the male approach that may be more cognitive focused, or action orientated. This can be very different from your average female interaction. Men can be, for a variety of reasons, naturally more boisterous, louder and have a stronger presence in social situations. Generally, this is not intended as threatening, yet can be perceived as such.

v. Be child-centred with men who are fathers. The child centred approach cuts through all other situations affecting the men's lives and helps them to redirect their attention to their child, e.g. 'How will that affect your child?'

vi. Men may be uncomfortable with programs that emphasise the provision of "support" because it suggests they are not coping. Use active terms like 'explore...', 'hear from other men talk about...'

The best approach for promoting programs to fathers is by word of mouth. Due to potential high levels of initial suspicion, fathers may ignore fliers and newspaper advertisements unless they are experiencing and wish to address a specific life crisis. When not in imminent crisis fathers may respond best to the recommendation of a program by someone they trust. Friends, family members, partners, colleagues, practitioners, doctors, other professionals and 'mates' can be respected gatekeepers who can influence men. Based upon the author's experience of delivering fathering programs, at least seventy five percent of referrals to many fathering programs rely on some form of recommendation by a respected gatekeeper.

When a program for men commences it is initially important to advertise in newspapers or fliers that create interest amongst the gatekeepers. The gatekeepers in men's lives may be the man's parents, grandparents, siblings, colleagues, religious leaders or uncles etc. Written promotions should clearly identify what will be gained by attending the program, doing words or active words, and emphasise that there will be an opportunity to hear other men's ideas. When referring a father to another program, it is best to refer them to a person who you recommend than an organisation. It will significantly increase the likelihood that they will follow up on the referral.

3. Initial contact and marketing

Family crisis can be a catalyst for fathers to reach out for support. Separated fathers are the single largest group of men who are known for their help-seeking behaviour and will actively look for support from services. During these crises, a short window period occurs where fathers may be more likely to accept help and support. If the crisis passes without obtaining support they may not engage again until the next crisis occurs, if at all. Consequently, when working with fathers, phone calls need to be answered or returned promptly to respond to this window of opportunity. Useful questions to engage separated fathers over the phone include:

i. When were they separated?
ii. What is the age and gender of the children?
iii. With whom do the children live?

iv.   Where have the father and mother lived since the separation?

v.   Current arrangements regarding contact?

vi.   Are there any court orders or Apprehended Violence Orders[161]?

These questions allow the practitioner to understand what the client needs and how they can respond. If the practitioner suggests solutions that have already been unsuccessful, the client can easily become frustrated. Using a solution-focused approach to counselling the practitioner can propose a range of options that include the client obtaining legal advice, or mediation etc. Self-care options may include visiting a General Practitioner, the local Community Health Centre or phoning Mensline Australia.

Recruiting fathers

Fathers are more likely to be involved in a program[162] when:

- Practitioners work in partnership with other services that are already engaged with fathers.
- The father's engagement is requested from the start as expected and important and included in the home visiting.
- Practitioners talk directly to individual fathers before seeking commitment to specific parenting groups.
- Sessions are provided at flexible times and in appropriate environments.
- Fathers who don't attend are followed up.
- The benefit to their child is repeatedly emphasised.
- Non-traditional fathers such as gay or bisexual couples are included as standard practice.
- The fathers' needs, including their mental health, are routinely assessed.
- The whole team seeks to (and is trained to) engage with fathers and build relationships with them (as they should do with mothers).
- The team regards the program as being as much for dads as for mums.
- Non-resident fathers are engaged with whenever possible;
- Mothers (and other fathers) are encouraged to think about the fathers' importance and help to recruit them.
- The mothers' ambivalence or resistance for involving the father is taken seriously.

Retaining fathers

Fathers are likely to find parenting interventions more rewarding when practitioners[163]:

- Clearly set out the goals and expectations of any parenting course.
- Consult with fathers about their goals for participation in the intervention, and tailor the program accordingly. Allow fathers and mothers to own the process for change, rather than the focus being on completing the program.
- Adopt a strengths-based approach which supports the father's capabilities rather than treating him as a resource.
- Help fathers create a baseline checklist of their involvement activities with their children, so they can see how they are progressing. Seek out feedback about the difference it makes within their family.
- Remind fathers of upcoming sessions (e.g. using text messaging) and follow up non-attenders.
- Introduce 'active' course elements (e.g. video playback, father-child activities) and ability to discuss things in smaller groups and move around the room.
- Create changes of mood/pace within the intervention (e.g. formal/informal; structured/unstructured; discussion/activity.
- Include information on fathers' roles in their child's development.
- Create opportunities for fathers (and mothers) to reflect on their understandings of gender, masculinity and care, in relation to their own fathers and other influences.
- Address couple-relationship issues and gender roles including the importance of uncles, step-fathers and grandfathers.
- Identify and provide 'space' to address loss (e.g. of children/ stepchildren /miscarriage/child protection issues).

4. Service provision

Men respond more positively when a range of different programs are offered such as telephone counselling, face-to-face counselling and group work and some choice is allowed. Some men will favour informal environments that have little structure, while others will desire a context where their concerns are specifically addressed. Other men will feel more comfortable in groups and others with face-to-face counselling. It is important for organisations to provide the widest range of contexts for working with men that are possible within their budget.

Men appreciate a basic structure that helps to reduce their concerns about what will be expected from them. Clearly identify what the client needs and what is expected of them when they use the program. Regularly review what is achieved and obtain feedback about the male client's opinions and reactions to their learning. At the end of the session, asking if the time together has been 'great', 'okay' or 'boring' is very useful for obtaining immediate feedback.

Fathers often appreciate a context where they feel valued and can have input into some of the decisions that affect their life. Without this level of regard, fathers may identify how to 'play the game' and use programs briefly to get what they want while holding themselves back from true involvement and commitment. When male clients need to make critical decisions, outline the available options with the belief that they can make an adequate choice.

Many fathers respond favourably when involved in a group program with other men who have experienced a similar situation. Their level of motivation and the availability of time will ultimately influence their attendance. It is important during the initial telephone engagement, to support the development of positive motivation. This is achieved by remaining child focused and emphasising that involvement in the program will allow them to learn from the situations that other men experience and enable them to manage their situation in a better way. After having some involvement, most men report that being involved in a group program has been a unique and rewarding experience. The length of group programs varies from 1-day information workshops to three hours a week for ten evenings. The range of groups includes information-based workshops, emotional support groups and psychoeducational groups.

Questions to consider in planning and delivering services[164]:

1. Where do fathers in the local community gather? Can you promote your program at these venues?

2. Consider fathers from culturally and linguistically diverse (CALD) communities: Where do they meet? Have you spoken to their community leaders? Can you work in partnership with them? What challenges will those men face as fathers?

3. What type of language is used in your promotional materials? Does it recognise the challenge for men to access help (i.e. courage to

change)? Do you use gendered language or refer to parents (which many communities view as code for 'mothers')? Does your promotional material state what the men will get out of the program and use active language to describe what will be occurring (i.e. avoid references to sit and listen)?

4. Are positive images displayed (photos not cartoon images) in the space or in your promotional materials? Are positive stories about fathers used and quotes about what other men have said regarding your program?

5. Does your program provide 'hands-on' learning experiences?

6. Is your program available outside of business hours?

The following Table 1 is a useful overview of engagement strategies, but it is by no means comprehensive.

Table 1: Reflection on useful strategies for engaging fathers

Context	Strategy	Reflection on the outcome
Safe environments	Where possible, go to where fathers are located on their 'turf". These could be sporting clubs, gyms, workplaces and other venues even pubs!	Fathering programs are best delivered when they look 'normal' and 'normal' men attend them. On your advertising, use logos of local businesses that support your program. This is a useful strategy especially when the men identify with the location as a culturally safe and appropriate place for them to meet. This is critical especially when working with Aboriginal fathers.
	Organise an event to attract fathers using fliers or other media. Events could be barbecues, family fun days, trips and sporting events. You could use local celebrities with male-friendly themes to attract them to your event.	

Obtain feedback	Involve the fathers in your services as partners or mentors in your organisation's overall strategic planning.	This is a critical strategy as 70% of fathers will access your program due to word-of-mouth recommendation. The start-up of new programs is always a challenge as not many people will be yet recommending them.
	Encourage and support the fathers you are already working with and seek their feedback on the services you are providing.	Road test your plans with a few fathers who you know from the local community. Always begin the discussion with the statement 'your honest feedback is valued'!
	The mother's ambivalence or resistance is taken seriously.	If your program mostly works with the primary parent at home during the day (often the mother), ensure that she consents to the contact that you having with the father. Any issues can be discussed in greater detail and her ambivalence or resistance is taken seriously.
Creating relevance	Invite and encourage the children to take part in engaging the fathers.	One of the best ways to promote fathering programs is through an invitation that the child creates and gives to their dad. Programs that adopt this approach routinely have a high attendance rate. Children who don't have a father can invite another important male role model in their life. The invitation process needs to be authentic.
	Invite and encourage the mothers to take part in engaging the fathers.	Routinely men report that their first attendance at a fathering program is due to the mother saying 'you need to go to this'! The involvement of the mothers can be useful as long as there is no conflict in the relationship. This approach can be adversely affected by the parent's prior relationship issues and expectations.
	Mothers (and other fathers) are encouraged to think about the fathers' importance and help to recruit them.	This approach is more likely to be successful as the mothers are not just relaying a message, but are involved in learning about the significant role fathers' play. This approach is likely to invest in whole-of-family changes that will impact on healthy relationships in the long term.

Strong engagement	The father's engagement is requested from the start as expected and important and included in the home visiting.	It is very important to establish clear expectations about what their involvement requires and also what it does not require. If they are not present when a home visit occurs, phone them to introduce yourself or provide an update on your last visit (see below). These discussions occur best when the focus is centred on the children and the father clearly understands he is viewed as a resource.
	If the father is not present at a home visit, regularly call them on their mobile to provide feedback and report any rapport building observations you have made regarding their children.	
	Practitioners talk directly to individual fathers before seeking commitment to a parenting course.	It is very important to initiate the development of a strong relationship with new male clients before the program commences. This initial introduction builds trust, respect, and rapport.
	Fathers who don't attend are followed up with a phone call.	This strategy needs to be tailored to the individual situation. It is useful to maintain strong lines of communication so you can regularly ask for feedback about the usefulness of the program or follow fathers up if they are not seen for a while.
Adopt a child centred approach	The benefit to their child is repeatedly emphasized.	This is essential when working with fathers. When the focus is directly on them, the discussion can be more difficult. When the discussion is on their children, men are often more free to share their opinions and reflections. This strategy is less likely to work is if they view their child in a very dismissive way and cannot recognise that they have needs.
Use a whole of program approach	The whole team seeks to (and is trained to) engage with fathers and build relationships with them (as they should do with mothers).	All of these strategies are vital for the involvement of dads to become mainstream part of a program's service delivery. The recognition that dads have a role to play in family life is central for their engagement. Otherwise they can be seen only as a problem. This often minimises resources for change for everyone.
	The team regards the program as being as much for dads as for mums.	
	The involvement of fathers is recognised in strategic plans and reported on in funding reports and annual reports.	

Emphasise inclusion	A broad definition of fathers is used that includes uncles, grandfathers, step fathers etc. even though different events/ programs may target different cohorts of fathers.	When a program is commencing keep your target group as broad as possible to ensure adequate numbers. At some stage it may be essential to have programs that target specific contexts due to the specific issues the fathers' experience. A good definition for many family services is 'our program supports mums, dads and other important caregivers in children's lives aged 0-8 years'.
	Non-traditional fathers such as gay or bisexual couples are included as standard practice.	
	Non-resident fathers are engaged with whenever possible.	
	Sessions are provided at flex-ible times and in appropriate environments.	Within funding constraints provide the wide-range of times in early evening and weekend time slot to see which are best for your community.

Engaging fathers at Childcare or Family Centres

Many early childcare centres report that many fathers seem ill-at-ease and want to escape (drop and run) when they come into the centre with their child[165]. They noticed that dads tend to drop their children off and go and only talk to staff when approached. The main barrier was identified as the fathers being unfamiliar with the centre, what is expected, and importance of the information exchange.

Engaging fathers at a Childcare Centre

Staff focused their attention on strengthening relationships with the 'drop and run' fathers.

'I intentionally maximized every opportunity to engage the dads in meaningful conversation that centred on their child's positive experiences at the centre. I noticed that interactions with one particular 'drop and run' dad were at a superficial level, often revolving around sport and weather. I attributed this to the pressing demands on my own time and the fathers' limited time at the centre. With an increased effort to 'catch up with' the dad before he left the centre, and by refocusing conversations around the child's experiences, I noticed that the relation-

ship between us improved. This also translated to improved relation-ships between the dad and other staff at the centre. The dad began staying longer at the centre, became more attuned to his child's interests, appeared more confident as a father and staff noticed the relationship between the father and child improved. I reconnected with this father following his child's commencement at school. The father recounted attending a school camp with his child and reporting this was a very positive experience for them both[166]

Ways to increase familiarity at childcare or family centres are:

- Use the first names of the fathers, as well as mothers, on invitations for special events.
- Hold information sessions in the evening, on the weekend, or at other times when fathers are more likely to be around (we recognise that this will vary from one locality to another).
- Have a dad's and a mum's display board that has information that directly targets either parent.
- Personally distribute booklets to all fathers and mothers, especially those who are not able to attend such a session.
- Greet fathers at the door of the setting every time they come with a focus on 'engaging' them. Keep the focus of the discussion on their child's experiences of the day. This will build a greater connection and help them to feel more welcomed and more familiar with the setting.
- Encourage the men to participate in routines with which they may not be familiar with when the father enters the setting (i.e. settling their children when they drop them off at the start of a session).

The following ways are useful for encouraging father involvement at a family or children's centre[167]:

- Create an environment that is friendly, inviting and comfortable for men.
- Hold "men at work' days at your centre where some of the men talk about their employment or volunteer work.
- Ask the children to write or colour-in an invitation for their father to attend a special event at the centre. Then ask them to give it to their dad. If the child does not have a father, encourage them to give to another important male in their life e.g. uncle, or pop.
- Involve men in the design and decoration of areas of the centre, including displaying photos of father involvement activities. Make men visible by attending the centre, or viewing posters, photos of past events at the centre.

- Encourage mothers to bring along their partners, boyfriends or brothers along to events and programs.
- Offer parent education programs for men on various topics including keeping children safe around the house, child development and communication. Mobilise the protective spirit within many men by holding a first aid workshop for fathers that focuses on infant CPR, handling your baby and home safety focus.
- Establish a fathers' group. Create opportunities for fathers to speak about their inner worlds and reflect on fatherhood.
- Create a male mentoring program or a volunteer program. These programs support informal involvement, practical approaches and the promotion of teamwork that allows them to interact with other fathers.
- Establish routines and rituals at your centre that involve and recognise fathers. Use questions that elicit his strength and insight into important issues like the welfare of his children.
- Invite fathers to participate in groups, panels or Management Committees.

Also try to[168]:

- Have practical activities for children and dads such as kite-making, billy-cart making and rough and tumble play opportunities.
- Use specific gendered language by referring to 'mothers and fathers and other important carers in the children's lives' instead of referring to general 'parents'.
- Make your message relevant to their key relationships – 'kids and dads' preparing for mothers' day. Be clear and specific and communicate early on in the relationship about your purpose for why you are involving dads (build trust and expectation).
- Create opportunities for staff to reflect on their own fathering and how they can bring fathers into the work.

Challenges for the sector

The challenges experienced by men's programs are shared with other community services. These challenges include:

- access to long term funding;
- improved supervision standards and practices;
- improved use of information obtained from evaluation processes;

- development of more strategic alliances and partnerships with other organisations;
- training, encouragement and mentoring of clients; and
- training and development of more male practitioners.

Change amongst fathers is occurring, which means that services need to follow. It is important to recognise that older men, male carers and many fathers are intuitive, even if this is different to the intuition that women demonstrate. The intuition is shown through:

- being conscious of the need for safety of themselves and others;
- focusing on the lifelong well-being and care for family members;
- supporting the notion of equality and mateship;
- valuing role models and mentoring of others; and
- quickly assessing the comfort level of new environments and whether these places will meet their needs.

The delivery of services to men is more successful and effective when a non-deficit approach is adopted. The Working with Fathers Checklist provides organisations with a tool to appraise their own context for delivering programs to men in family relationships. The assumptions embedded in the checklist, reflect the non-deficit perspective and identify that most men:

- Act intuitively – they quickly tune into feelings of safety and comfort. They will make rapid assessments about whether a program/service seems friendly and useful or judgemental and critical.
- Place a considerable importance on their relationships with their children.
- Appreciate clear rules and expectations on which they can rely and trust that other people will do what they promise.
- Respect and value feedback that is delivered in a non-threatening respectful manner.
- Use anger as a defence to protect themselves or others or to maintain or regain control of a perceived unsafe or threatening situation.

The Working with Fathers Checklist

The Working with Fathers Checklist captures the key issues discussed in this chapter and contains four key areas that allow organisations to assess and improve engaging fathers across the areas of environment, language, initial contact and marketing, and service provision.

Scoring

At the end of the Working with Men Checklist, there is a scoring system that allows organisations to measure their results. The Checklist Scale converts answers into a score by multiplying the number of 'sometimes' responses by two; the number of 'regularly' responses by three and number of 'not often' responses remain the same. These numbers are tallied to create a final score.

The scoring guide is below:

Final Score between...	Suggested response
40 - 65	Significant work needs to be done to improve the organisational support and range of service provision that attracts and retains fathers in your service.
66 - 80	Your organisation could spend more time in addressing key issues and policies that can allow for the further development and support of staff who work with men in your agency. It may be useful to consult your existing staff about ways that your organisation can improve its services to fathers.
81 - 100	A good score that indicates your organisation has been working actively in becoming 'male friendly'. It might be useful to spend more time getting feedback from your current male clients and to further improve your service delivery to fathers.
101 - 120	An excellent score that demonstrates that your agency is continually learning and developing its service provision that targets fathers and families.

Engaging men constructively in social welfare services can be challenging and very rewarding. Often when men engage with a service that they perceive as supportive, respectful, and non-judgemental and validating of their experiences, they will bring enthusiasm and energy to make changes and grow. Men will have a greater interest for contacting a program when someone they trust has personally recommended it to them.

Many fathers enter new situations with a significant level of suspicion. These suspicions need to be alleviated by practitioners building trust and creating a relaxed environment which contains positive images of males and providing services relevant to men's lives.

The Working with Fathers Checklist is a useful tool for organisations to appraise their working with men practice by reviewing their environment, language, initial contact, marketing and service provision.

Table 2: Checklist for organisations working with fathers

Environment	Not often	Sometimes	Regularly
How often does your centre…?			
Display posters that depict positive male images			
Provide accessibility for car parking or public transport			
Hold special events or groups that are held outdoors (i.e. parks, BBQ's)			
Distribute male friendly reading material (booklets or brochures promoting positive messages for men)			
Have male staff or other male clients, who could be noticed by other men entering your centre for the first time			
Display photos of centre activities (with men and children) in the centre			
How often does your organisation…?			
Provide services and have events/groups outside normal working hours (After 5.00pm and on weekends)			
Actively support all staff (regardless of gender) to work with male clients			
Review policies that specifically identify positive ways of working with and better target male clients			
Maintain policies that identify when men are included or excluded from receiving services			
Employ male practitioners to work directly with clients			
Language used - How often does your program…?			
Involve fathers in discussing important family issues			
Use clear and simple language rather than jargon			
Talk about issues honestly and directly, even when the client is emotional			
Link family issues with a child focused approach			
Challenge inappropriate language and behaviour without immediately withdrawing your service			

Use *respectful language* such as 'mother of the child' rather than 'ex' when describing the mother			
Avoid stereotypes and generalisations that all men are violent or perpetrators of domestic violence or child abuse			
Affirm the role fathers play with their children and families			
Use open body language …e.g. Shake hands (positive body contact, non-threatening and validating)			
Use intermittent eye contact especially when the client has a high degree of anxiety or emotion			
Aware of male 'personal space' which may be different depending on the gender of the practitioner			
Use non-deficit language in flyers and other promotional material. Non-deficit language reinforces the ideas that men can commit, choose, have capacity to relate with children, capacity to make day to day decisions, care, change, create, connect, communicate and can form lasting and healthy attachments with their children/partner			
Initial Contact and Marketing - How often does your program….?			
Identify clear purposes for having barbeques, meetings, counselling sessions, gatherings and groups in your advertising			
Use 'doing' language and 'active' words in your promotion			
Have clients recommending your program to other men			
Use the local media to promote your program			
Give clients choices about available services with clear explanations about their options at point of intake			
Use appropriate informality at the beginning of meetings/groups/gatherings			
Service provision			
How often does your program…?			

Have a clear context, guidelines, focus, and aim for clients attending your programs			
Encourage interaction and connections between clients			
Separate the person from the behaviour when dealing with male clients			
Allow clients to provide feedback and influence the program content			
Have review points and clear ending points for clients involved in your service			
Present a variety of choices when working with men			
Model non-competitiveness and celebrate small successes, fairness, cooperation and equity			
Have clear rules and expectations that are relevant to client needs			
Talk with clients about challenging tasks they need to do and provide fathers with coaching about how they can be completed			
Recognise that male clients have something valuable to contribute			
Use appropriate techniques to reduce the suspicion and concerns that male clients sometimes have when they attend a program			
Actively request feedback from male clients and members of the community about how approachable your service is			
Sub-total of Points			
New Total for Column, then add the columns together.	**Multiply by 1**	**Multiply by 2**	**Multiply by 3**
Final Total i.e. Column 1+2+3 =			

Final Total	**i.e. Column 1+2+3 =**	

Calculate your final score using the above method and compare to the scoring outcomes.

Chapter 5:

Generativity – A force for change

'It is human to have a long childhood; it is civilised to have an even longer childhood. Long childhood makes a technical and mental virtuoso out of man, but it also leaves a lifelong residue of emotional immaturity in him.'

Erik Homburger Erikson (1902-1994)

Introducing the concept of generativity

Erik and Joan Erikson built their psychosocial stages of human development on a series of dyads, or opposing personality traits. People think of themselves as: optimistic or pessimistic, independent or dependent, emotional or unemotional, adventurous or cautious, leader or follower, and aggressive or passive.

The Eriksons' became aware of the massive influence of culture on behaviour and placed more emphasis on the social impact that the external world has on an individual's development such as siblings, peers, employment, parenting or economic depressions or wars. This was based in part on the study of Sioux Indian reservations. They felt the course of an individual's development was determined by interaction of the body (genetic biological programming), mind (psychological) and cultural (ethos) influences[169].

Based on working with traditional cultural groups, the Erikson's organised life into eight stages that extend from birth to death (many developmental theories only cover childhood). Since adulthood covers a span of many years, its stages are divided into the experiences of young adults, middle-aged adults and older adults. While the actual ages may vary considerably from one stage to another, the ages seem to be appropriate for most people. The Eriksons' divided the lifecycle up into eight life stages that are still relevant today and especially when working with fathers.

Life stages of development

1. Infancy: birth to 18 months
    Trust vs mistrust
    Basic strengths: drive and hope

2. Early childhood: 18 months to 3 years
    Autonomy vs shame
    Basic strengths: self-control, courage and will

3. Play age: 3 to 5 years
    Initiative vs guilt
    Basic strength: purpose

4. School age: 6 to 12 Years
    Industry vs inferiority
    Basic strengths: method and competence

5. Adolescence: 12 to 18 Years
    Identity vs role confusion
    Basic strengths: devotion and fidelity

6. Young adulthood: 18 to 35
    Intimacy and solidarity vs isolation
    Basic strengths: affiliation and love

7. Middle adulthood: 35 to 55
    Generativity vs self-absorption or stagnation
    Basic strengths: production and care

8. Late adulthood: 55 to death
    Integrity vs despair
    Basic strengths: wisdom

Central to Erikson's ideas are the belief that, somewhere along the way, the strength of the human spirit can be ignited and deficits overcome. This is encapsulated in the concept of generativity. Generativity refers to the capacity to care for the next generation and demands the ability to give something of yourself to another person. Generativity is powered by the motivation to 'invest one's substance in forms of life and work that will outlive the self' [170]. Generativity is best understood as a persons' behaviour in response to an external situation that triggers feelings of vulnerability. The generative stage of life is the primary developmental task of adulthood. As the seventh life stage, it's successful navigation demands lessons to be learnt during the previous six stages.

Generativity has three major expressions in society; biological, parental, and societal. Biological generativity is the birth and care of a new generation. It involves nursing and attending to the immediate needs of a newborn. This life experience provides an initial motivation for someone to reflect on their life goals and aspirations and what is required through caring for that newborn. Parental generativity involves a wider developmental and relational view of the fullness of childhood and young adulthood. Parents adapt their care in response to children's changing needs. The generative object is the child and their nurturance, care, development, discipline and learning of their own social, family and cultural context. Societal generativity is a person's care and nurturance towards others throughout all the community. While children are often the strongest expression of generativity in people's lives, the societal connection can be observed through:

- Service clubs, Lifeline, SES, Rural Fire Service;
- Volunteering and mentoring;
- Spirituality;
- Sport – if your involvement provides rewards beyond the immediate reward of competition and exercise;
- Employment context – if you identify the importance of making a difference through your job;
- Friends (other people you identify with in a similar situation);
- Music;
- Artistic expressions;
- Other key relationships, particularly where vulnerability may exist e.g. a sibling with special needs;
- Wider community interests;
- Dogs/animals/pets; and
- Gardening.

Generativity has only recently been applied in the community services context. Generativity is equally important yet differentially expressed in men and women's lives. The generative (7th) stage is when people focus on the greater impact they have on their immediate world and find practical ways that this is fulfilled. In women's lives it is discussed and practiced much more from childhood and is strongly expressed in nurturing and intimacy. In men's lives, it is less spoken about from a younger age, and is strongly expressed in how they are viewed within their community (those people they significantly identify with), their workplace and their connection to their children.

Due to the importance of generativity in psychosocial development it can be particularly valuable for practitioners working with men. The generative fathering framework is a model for understanding the non-deficit approach to fathering[171]. Generative fathering is described as '... fathering that meets the needs of children by working to create and maintain a developing valuable relationship with them'[172].The concept of generative fathering is compatible with a Resource Theory of Fathering[173]. The Resource Theory of Fathering argues that fathers are more likely to contribute to the development of the relational, spiritual and ethical needs of their children when they possess either an implicit or explicit understanding of the significant and long-term role they play in their children's lives. Fundamental to fathers' confidence and understanding in their fathering ability is having enough time, and having the responsibility to provide one-on-one care of their child that is independent of the mother or any other care-giver.

This story outlines how one father put generativity into practice.

> *David is a father who has not had much meaningful contact with his two sons throughout their 12 years of life. Having experienced a great deal of trauma in his younger years, he has a limited ability to socialise or play with his children. His great desire is to be a better father than his father was to him. He finds this difficult as he has survived intense violence all his life and has resorted to violence many times to deal with any conflict in his adult years. During his participation in the group, David was enduring an ongoing court drama with the NSW Department of Family and Community Services to have a meaningful role in the life of his children. The children were being removed from their mother and he was struggling to put a case forward to become their full-time carer. David desperately wanted their life to be better than his own. One of the educational sessions covered a concept outlining the*

limitations of what we can control, as compared to what we can influence, and letting go of what is outside our control and influence.

David left the program that night enthusiastic about how he could use this idea at his next court date. The following week he returned to the group a very different man: wearing cleaner clothes, holding his body more erect, taking more pride in his appearance and being much happier. He told the story of attending the court the preceding week. The mother of his children had attempted to engage him in a conflict in the court grounds by being verbally abusive and aggressive, and he had refused to engage with her. He had acknowledged to himself that he could not control her, or what she was saying, so he had walked away. This was an achievement.

When the court was sitting, the mother again attempted to engage him in conflict by staring and mouthing swear words at him. He continued to ignore her. When the court proceedings were not going his way and inaccurate information about him was being put forward, he did not react as he had in the past, by trying to use threats and loud language to control the court. Rather, he decided to let it go (as best he could) as he could not control it and instead attempted to influence the court by his 'good' behaviour. Although quite proud of himself for the change in his behaviour in a very stressful situation, the best for David was yet to come.

The case was adjourned. Before he left the court, David approached the solicitor acting for his children and said, "I know you don't like me and that's okay." He then added, "I've been watching and listening to you and you seem like a good person who has the best interests of my sons at heart. I just want to let you know I appreciate what you are trying to do for my boys." The solicitor, in a spontaneous gesture, offered David the opportunity to spend a short time with his eldest son. Not having seen his son in over four weeks, David accepted enthusiastically. He spent 20-minutes with his boy which he otherwise would not have had. David was ecstatic at this good fortune. This generous gesture by the solicitor continues to have a positive impact on David's life because he has experienced the rewards of learning new ways of dealing with conflict.

Besides being applied to human development for men, women and fathering, generativity has had a significant contribution to understanding healthy ageing. The Harvard Study of Adult Development reviewed societal trends in the last 50 years and concluded that generativity is the best indicator for social-emotional wellness. The study concluded that the old were put on the earth to nurture the young[174]. However, generativity is not about just giving to others, but is also found in the receiving. A matched study[175] identified that similar generative impacts existed in alcohol recovery research using the Alcoholics Anonymous (AA) approach. This research indicated that the best predictor for sobriety occurred when people invested something of themselves into helping someone else (being a sponsor). This occurred independent of how many AA meetings they attended.

How generativity works

Generativity involves caring for or influencing someone external to you or supporting the development of the next generation. Specifically, generativity is a force that motivates an individual to connect with and support a key relationship in their lives (see Figure 3). Generativity is best mobilised when a key relationship has a greater perceived vulnerability than the client themselves. The perceived vulnerability of the person in the key relationship can motivate the individual, through empathy, to invest in and support the other.

How Generativity Works

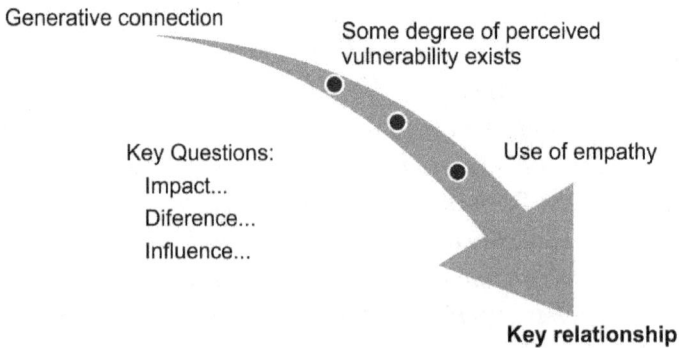

Generative connection

Some degree of perceived vulnerability exists

Key Questions:
Impact...
Diference...
Influence...

Use of empathy

Key relationship

Figure 3: How generativity works

Generative connections may be expressed in different ways. Table 3 presents the dimensions that generative connections may be expressed along; developmental, relational, spiritual, and ethical. Someone may have strength within 1-2 elements, while being weak within another.

Table 3: The key dimensions of generativity

Developmental	The process of development, growth and progress in others, interests or the broader community.
Relational	The expression and interpretation of messages within close relationships. The two major requirements are time and proximity. Many fathers are usually able to get those two elements right. Regardless of how many ways there are to look after one's child, the presence of love is the most important requirement.
Spiritual	Spirituality involves the deepest values and meanings by which people live. It requires someone to view life's opportunities and challenges through a larger lens where the issue is beyond our own immediate needs or interests.
Ethical	Nurtures self and others in equitable, fair and just ways when dealing with challenges. Although pragmatically flexible according to the situation and times, the ethical response expresses self-imposed high standards of public conduct.

An individuals' generative response to perceived vulnerability within the key relationship may not be a universally positive one (see Table 4). In fact, neutral or negative generative responses can also be triggered. Often in family violence situations, men will not see their partner in a generative way. Domestic violence is driven by the man's need to control and dominate his partner. However, men will often have a generative connection towards their children.

If the client has a negative response, they offer little to the key relationship and could be quite harmful unless watched. If they have a neutral response, there is opportunity for change and the development of a positive response. If they have a positive response, they have some key strengths that will be useful for the child and help create safety in the situation.

Table 4: Client's response to the perceived vulnerability

Client's response to the perceived vulnerability in the key relationship	
Negative response	The vulnerability and needs experienced in the key relationship is likely to be rejected or even exploited for personal gain.
Neutral response	Little attention is given to the vulnerability and needs experienced in the key relationship, with little insight or need for a personal response.
Positive response	There is an interest in and positive response towards the vulnerability and needs experienced in the key relationship.

In this story, a father, Tim (fictitious name), uses generativity to make changes in his life:

Tim, aged 38, had to battle with the child protection agency to become the primary carer of his child. Over 12 months, he attended several community-based fathering workshops and programs. The agency's psychologist completed two psychological reports in that period and stated: "In 20 years of clinical experience I have never seen anyone change as much as Tim." Tim's determination and dedication to using these ideas and new learning was apparent to many people.

Just prior to becoming the full-time carer of his child, Tim said: "Taking my daughter home will be the best experience in my whole life. It's like winning the World Cup. Everything else in life has always been taken away from me – that's why I'm paranoid. I have had to learn patience." He also commented on his involvement in the fathers' group: "Thanks for your help. I don't think I would have made it without the group. This group has impacted on me. It speaks about life the way it is. It wasn't pen and paper stuff. My dream has come true. It is achievable if you are determined. A lot of times you can't see the end of the road, but you just have to keep going."

Understanding the generative perspective is useful when working with fathers because it:

- Provides a strength-based framework to understand many men's focus on the external world rather than the internal world of their feelings.
- Emphasises the significance of their relationship with the child that has hopes/ dreams and aspirations for the child regardless of the amount of time they spend with them.

- Values the importance of men seeing that the parenting experience may require greater responsibility that contains a message that you need to often give up something for yourself to gain something.
- Allows you to appreciate the challenge that stepfathers may have to be generative towards the new children in the relationship and not just focus on their connection to the partner.
- Provides a framework of tools to use when working with fathers.

Practicing generativity is central to men's own sense of self-esteem and growth. The generative approach converts the father's anxiety into genuine concern that leads to a commitment to have a positive influence in his child's life. Rather than being a selfless act, it can be seen as adopting a partly self-serving role – investing now to benefit in the future.

A father called Mensline Australia and talked about feeling suicidal due to the loss of his children and family. After a 40-minute discussion the man was more stable and no longer feeling suicidal. The counsellor, in summing up, asked: 'What was important about this discussion?' The man replied: 'Do you know what the most helpful thing was? While we were talking, I looked down and saw my dog sitting at my feet. I realised that I was still needed to take care of him.'

Generative interventions for fathers

Practitioners who use the generative perspective are likely to be better at engaging men, reduce their suspicion about community welfare/health organisations and increase their help-seeking behaviour and motivation.

Generative questioning create a shared focus on past experience, the present context and the future aspirations. They elicit a person's role and responsibility to key external relationships. These questions have a powerful impact when working with men and women. However, a central role for men are often defined by active generative responses such as involvement in sporting groups, community service, the workplace or connection with their children. These questions build on the impact of the generative role such as the story below:

Ahab (not his real name) has a significant criminal background and has had significant involvement with the criminal system and Probation and Parole (P&P). He has had a poor response to P&P supervision, with many Orders resulting in breach action. His current offence is DV related. When the client was transferred to another P&P Officer, they were having a very busy and frustrating day. Despite the case file being three lever arch files thick, she had only enough time to read through the recent material. She noticed that he was a father of two children and the only positive comments were several comments on case notes from other P&P officers that indicated he was a 'good dad'. Ahab was a large man with tattoos all over his arms. When the interview commenced that morning, the P&P Officer commenced with her usual welcome and introduction.

*Ahab's first words were 'well I ain't f***** happy to be here'. His body was so tense it was shaking. The P&P Officer simply gathered all his files up and indicated that she did not have the time for games and should he choose, he can leave now. His breach matter would come up in court in a few weeks' time. Just before she left the room she turned and said to him "it was a shame to put so much at risk - given his history he could well be looking at doing time again". She stated, "it would be a shame, because what I have read indicated you are a great dad, and you are risking important special times with your children". His whole demeanour changed instantly - she could physically see it - his face, body and hands. His tone softened. They started the interview all over, with much better results. It was the first time this client had seriously addressed the Orders and went on to complete most of them.*

The generative perspective supports the definition of 'social fathering' as a key point for engaging and working alongside a wider range of men in the child's life. Adopting a social view of fathering is important not only because the term is inclusive, but because its use implies recognition of the diversity of roles men as fathers play in the lives of children in contemporary families today[176]. The more men are responsive to their child's needs, the more they will be involved in social expressions of generative care within their local community.

Below is a list of general questions that can be used with fathers. There may be other additional considerations required from fathers from special communities including CALD fathers, separated fathers, and fathers with a history of family violence, which are covered in their specific chapters.

- Find out the man's preferred name and introduce yourself.
- Find out how many children he has, their age and their special interests.

- Build a connection around how your work context is relevant to him and the context of his children (remember, he is unlikely to express a need for support and help).
- Assume, and discuss with him how it shows in his responses, that he has the desire and the ability to:
  ○ Commit - the physical and ongoing support a father provides and his awareness and involvement with a child throughout their life-time.
  ○ Choose - the capacity to make day to day decisions for the children that meet their needs.
  ○ Care - the ability to attend to the important transitions in a child's life and provide the optimal conditions that maximise their growth.
  ○ Change - the ability to adapt as children grow older and the father matures in his relationship with the children.
  ○ Create - the creation of resources for material comfort and the resolution of problems to allow opportunities for the development of emotional well-being.
  ○ Connect - the ability to form lasting and healthy attachments with a child. These will change over time to meet the child's evolving needs.
  ○ Communicate - the capacity to relate with children by sharing meaningfully with them, verbally and non-verbally.
- Discover the man's way of expressing his connection with the children (using the above abilities).
- Explore opposites or tensions – what helps/blocks and what is valuable or a distraction to achieving the above.
- Normalise experiences he has and validate the strengths men bring to parenting.
- Amplify the significance of positive choices he makes in his child's life.
- Discuss what the role of fathering means today. What parts of the role are important to him?
- Build the metaphor of walking alongside him in the work you do. Find out how this may be helpful to him rather than telling him what to do.

If appropriate, ask some of the following generative questions[177]. Generative questioning may be introduced with the statement, for example: "I would like to find out about some of your experiences with your child (who is called Sam) and what those experiences mean to you and Sam."

- "Can you tell me about the most enjoyable experience you ever had with Sam? What meaning does that experience have for you now?"
- "Can you tell me about an experience when you felt especially close emotionally to Sam? What meaning does that experience have for you now?"
- "Can you tell me about an experience when you cared for and nurtured Sam? What did you learn about nurturing children from that experience?"
- "Can you tell me about an experience when you felt especially distant emotionally from Sam when he/she needed you to be there for him/her? What meaning does that experience have for you now?
- "What was the most painful experience you ever had with Sam? What meaning does that experience have for you now?"
- "Are there any particular things that help you to be the kind of father to Sam that he/she needs you to be?"
- "Are there any particular things that prevent you from being the kind of father to Sam that he/she needs you to be?"
- "Can you tell me about any important sacrifices you have made in your life that demonstrate how much you care about Sam?"

If relevant, to discuss potential generative connections and family safety issues, it may also be useful to ask:

- "Who or how do you protect others in your life?"
- "Who do you keep safe?"
- "What happens when the protection of others is misused?"
- "What is the difference between keeping someone safe and controlling them?"
- "When does protecting someone become abusive?"
- "How do you keep yourself safe?"

Young people are still exploring their own purpose and meaning in life, so their generative connections are often in their infancy and changeable. A key focus is shifting their focus on safety from only themselves to that of others:

- Find out who they trust and are close to with immediate friends, girlfriends, at your centre and in their wider life. Safely discuss important relationships that have had or still are central in their life.
- Identify what they have learnt and continue to learn in those relationships.
- Build the metaphor of walking alongside them in the work you do.

Find out how this may be helpful to them (use perceived equality) for guidance.

- How many children do they have, their ages, do they live with them? If not what orders are in place and when they last had contact with their children?
- What would they like to change about those relationships?

Other generative interventions a practitioner can use are:

- Focus on active and practical ways of being in the world and having an influence and impact on others. Use questions that ask about 'impact', 'difference' or 'influence' e.g. "How does your response have an impact on your son?" Discuss how they have an impact, who they influence and who they respect. Also, who are the people who have an impact on, influence and respect them?
- Build on a future focus: how their impact, influence and level of respect with their key relationships will be in the future. Ask "What do you want to do more of?"
- Challenge perceptions of hopelessness and focus on active responses they still make that look out for or care for other important people in their life. Ask "How do you want to be seen?"
- Acknowledge the challenge of being a reasonable man in an unreasonable situation.
- Discuss clear expectations of how you will work together and what is required and reduce the fear of the unknown. Identify relationship changes:
  - "What has changed?"
  - "What has not changed?"
  - "What do you want to achieve?"
- Build on discussions that highlight key relationships and the person's significant hopes and fears/anxiety (yearning vs challenges).
- Identify and name key values that are conscious, purposeful and can help to widen the range of choices they can use in response. This identifies and builds on primary motivations.

Case study

A father at a training workshop told this story that captures the developmental expression of generativity: *It was November and the family was preparing the house for the approaching bushfire season. This involved cleaning the gutters of a single story house. He was on a ladder leaning against the house while the gutters were cleaned. His five-year old son was below playing on the grass. It was his son's 5th birthday that day. His boy said to him, 'Dad, I don't feel like I'm five.' The father came down and sat with his son and talked to him. Soon he asked his son to come up the ladder and to sit on the roof while we continued to work. The father was always right next to him, surrounding him and shielding him in safety. As the young boy sat quietly on the roof, with the ladder and his dad acting as a barrier, the son looked around and saw his backyard in a very different way. The mother, came outside and was very upset at the risk of their son being on the roof. She demanded that he brought back down immediately. The father complied. It was later in the morning that the son came up to his dad and whispered, 'I now feel like I'm five!'*

Challenges to generative connections

There are four key challenges that may have an adverse impact on the generative stage: self-absorption; stagnation, depression, and other mental health issues (including alcohol/drug dependency); 'generative chill' anxiety; and the juggling of multiple demands.

Self-absorption

When men are too self-focused, narcissistic or self-absorbed, they find it difficult to have empathy for others or respond to other people's needs. Self-absorption may occur due to beliefs about entitlement or a man's emotional responses causing him to primarily focus on his own needs being met.

Stagnation, depression and other mental health issues

Mental health and/or addiction problems have a significant effect on men's motivation to be involved in support services. Some fathers drop out of support programs due to these issues. Others use the experience as part of their change program. To meet the challenge of supporting a participant's recovery, programs need to be flexible enough to allow longer-term involvement. Alcohol or drug misuse often skews a person's perception of their needs and what response is required in a certain situation.

Peter is a young stepfather with a dependence on marijuana. One week he said: *"I gave up pot for three days, but I have had a challenging week. I'm trying to do the right things, but no-one gives me any credit." He talked about the challenge of the family and the social context he lives in: "I want to say 'f... it' and leave. But the love you have stops you. The kids really love me. "It's been my life. I smoke a few cones (marijuana), drink beer and watch TV. I can't get a job as I need to learn to cope first with hassles at home. Dad overdosed last year. Since then, things have gone downhill." He went on to talk about the daily battle he has regarding his choices: "I don't want to walk out of the front door because the neighbours will say, 'Come and have a smoke.'" After four months, Peter still resisted seeing a drug and alcohol counsellor and he recently left his relationship. This is the tragedy that often impacts on families where there are addiction issues. It is important for programs to be able to work simultaneously with recovery, relationship and child protection issues.*

Generative chill

Extreme threats to an adult's parental generativity can cause 'generative chill', a type of anxiety resulting from a perceived or real danger of losing the child or children they have helped to create[178]. It is likely that brief or extended threats to generativity will have a significant impact on a father's selfhood[179]. Family breakdown presents separated fathers with a threat that often results in depression.

Generative chill is a useful concept for understanding how fathers disengage from their children. The challenge is how men can rebuild this generative connection. Professionals and close family members may want to help men deal with the pain of their family separation, but it is the father's timing alone that will ultimately dictate when he is open to rebuilding connection, engagement or reunion with his child.

Generative chill[180] is described as the anxious awareness people experience arising from the threatened loss of the relationship with one's child. The reaction men have to family separation will be influenced by how they deal with this experience. When separation is managed well, generative chill is a motivation that creates a stronger father/child relationship. When separation is managed poorly, generative chill becomes depression, despair and disengagement. The generative fathering framework supports a process for rebuilding engagement post relationship-breakdown by identifying new roles that separated fathers can play in their children's lives. The primary roles that fathers have played in the family before the family separation occurred may need to be re-adjusted e.g. providing financial security or being the protector (while this role may not exist, it still provides a high level of motivation for men). Secondary roles that traditionally may have had less prominence, such as cooking for the children, reading stories and talking about ordinary life experiences, will become more important and rewarding in the new post-separation relationship. Generativity in the context of separated fathers is discussed in detail in Chapter 6.

While the reassessment of these roles will be difficult, the new roles used post-separation are often more rewarding and relationship-enriching. The following case is an example of this reassessment of a new role:

Mike (fictitious name) is a separated father in his early 40s who came very close to throwing himself in front of a train due to depression. The relationship problems in his life and lack of contact with his children were a continual struggle for him. He was often overwhelmed by the depression and his inability to change his post separation parenting situation. He eventually attended a father's group and spoke about it being a vital place where he could be himself regardless of how the week had gone.

He stated: "It has been a good 12 months. I have received good support that has helped me to keep sane while I battle to see my son. Attending the group has turned around my whole relationship with my older son. I still play the memory game with my boy and he loves it. I feel a lot closer emotionally to him and understand why he reacts that way too." He added: "The kids are my main priority. I now accept that Sue and I have finished our relationship. I am sleeping a lot better now." He changed his employment and moved to a new area, and he values all the child contact opportunities that are possible.

Juggling multiple demands

Men and women often juggle a variety of roles and pressures in the normal course of the day. Men, however, may not choose to demonstrate generative responses due to many practical barriers such as work/ time constraints and the stress experienced as a result of meeting these competing demands. The best response to review the balance of life's demands is to be transparent about the available choices and possible consequences. Professionals may then discuss with men the alternative choices they can have and those with the best possible outcomes can be selected. There are many examples mentioned in a recent book titled, *Fathering from the Fast Lane* by Bruce Robinson. In his book, he discusses ways in which fathers can negotiate with their employer to attend significant events in their children's lives and meet the demands of work[181].

CHAPTER 6:

GENERATIVITY AND DISENGAGED SEPARATED FATHERS

Separation is a key challenge to generativity in men's lives. It is in separation that the father's role in being a protector and provider may significantly change. When these roles are redefined in a useful way, the generative connection with their child or children may strengthen as the time spent together is often valued more preciously and less likely to be taken for granted. This chapter focuses on the challenging context where fathers disengage from their child and how that reconnection may occur. It discusses ways to improve engagement with separated fathers who desire a reconnection with their chid. Strategies are identified that support separated fathers to re-engage with their child when it is safe from the impact of domestic violence.

What motivates fathers to disengage from their children?

Post-separation, some fathers experience disengagement from their children and have little involvement or contact time. Disengagement occurs through either circumstances, court orders, or by choice. Estimates from the Australian Bureau of Statistics suggest that in 1997 approximately 30% of children saw their non-residential parent less than once a year or never; by 2009–10, this had decreased to 26%[182]. It is estimated that 4% of children rarely or never see their non-resident parent (typically their father)[183]. Several reasons that that fathers rarely see their children have been identified including, child protection or domestic violence, conflict with the mother of their children, and issues about how the father copes with the legal and social issues surrounding the separation[184]. '

After family separation occurs, children benefit from some level of involvement with both parents as long as an unacceptable risk to the child does not exist. Over the past decade, there has been a steady increase in separated fathers being more involved with contact or care of their children. The Care-time Arrangements of Child/ren Study[185] reported that often it was the younger children who never saw their father. Consistent with other research, the report found that when fathers have limited face-to-face time with the child occurs, there is little time to deepen bonding, develop a stronger commitment to them. These limited contact situations often involve complex personal dynamics, conflict and or domestic violence. Mothers that reported the father never saw the child were more likely to report high levels of conflict and fear of the other parent; experience family violence before or during pregnancy; or had mental health issues or substance abuse before separation. The same study identified that the challenges for fathers to move from no contact to some contact primarily depended upon the child's age; distance between the two homes and the quality of the inter-parental relationships[186]. Improved contact was more likely to occur when children were aged 3-11 years. It was less likely to occur with toddlers and teenagers. The quality of interpersonal relationships was strongly impacted by high levels of conflict and fear compared to friendly, cooperative or distant relationships.

After family separation occurs, non-resident parents' contact with children will vary as the children change and grow[187]. Parkinson and Smyth (cited in Smyth[188]) found that 75% of non-resident fathers would like to have more contact with their children. The hope that non-resident fathers might have more contact with their children was also supported by 40% of resident mothers.

Yet, it is not uncommon for fathers to feel disengaged from their children post-separation. Disengagement can involve an active or unconscious decision by a parent to have minimal involvement physically or emotionally with their children. They might disengage due to:
- increased geographic distance between them and their children;
- increased economic demands;
- new family responsibilities;
- their inability to deal with their own anger or the mother's anger;
- feeling it is in the best interests of the child/ren as they will be exposed to less conflict; and/or

- high to extreme level of father-child alienation.

The decision to limit contact with one's children is neither straightforward nor easy for men to make. Kruk[188] interviewed forty men about the reasons why they disengaged from their child or children. Of the men who disengage from having contact with their children, 90% of these men disconnect due to the pain and frustration that arises when they have contact with their children (see Table 5).

Table 5: Reason separated fathers disengaged from contact with children

	Percentage of men	Number of men
Contact difficulties	90%	(36)
Father's decision to cease contact	33%	(13)
Practical difficulties to making contact happen (distance, finances, shift work schedules)	28%	(11)
Child(ren) not wanting contact	18%	(7)
Legal orders prohibiting contact due to family violence	16%	(6)
Early pattern of no contact (influencing future contact)	5%	(2)

Non-residential fathers' disengagement from their children should not be interpreted only as a lack of interest in their children, or the end result of previous difficult father-child relationships. Kruk[189] stated that psychological factors related to fathers' unresolved grief and inability to adapt to child absence, role loss, and the constraints of the 'visiting' relationship, are significant factors in their disengagement. Fathers' lack of help-seeking behaviour further intensifies the grief and increases the impact of the losses involved with the separation (i.e. loss of child relationship, partner relationship and increased job pressure). Common reasons for fathers' disengagement are discussed in detail below.

Physical factors

Relocation: Children in some cases may be immediately relocated by the mother to outside the city, state or even country where they resided prior to the separation. In Australia, at least one in four non-resident parents (mostly fathers) lives a significant distance (more than 500 kilometres) from their children[189]. The amount of contact non-resident parents have with their children is strongly influenced by the distance they live apart. In recent times, many separated fathers have been much more proactive with seeking the assistance of the Court in returning the children to their usual place of residence until formal arrangements can be decided by the parents or the Court.

Reduced standard of living: Fathers may have to accept less than adequate accommodation that may not be suitable for their children. Some men are forced to live with friends, family of origin, in bed sits, backyard granny flats, etc.

Financial hardship: Some fathers report finding it difficult to cover the costs of contact with their children due to the demands of child support, legal fees and re-establishment costs after separation occurs. While women and children are more likely to experience financial hardship after separation/divorce, a significant number of men are not in a strong economic position, particularly men living alone[190].

Adversarial nature of legal processes

Legal processes that exacerbate conflict: Direct communication between the parents may be minimal when communication is channelled through legal representatives. The non-compliance by either parent with agreements or Court Orders can lead to exasperation from a parent who may be unaware of the enforcement options available, or unable or unwilling to re-enter the legal process to gain compliance.

Fathers who are finding the separation process difficult benefit from accurate information which is understandable to them. Some fathers may feel a sense of betrayal by the system, and can have feelings expressed through statements such as 'where are my rights?' or 'the system is supporting her'. The key here is to work with the father's instinctive nature for protecting and supporting his children. When he is seen as confrontational or aggressive towards the mother, the safety he desires for his children is compromised. This is an important realisation for the father as he develops a child-focused solution approach where the safety of the child is essential. However, this may be limited in domestic violence situations where the father's desire is to control the mother's responses and actions.

The use of Family Relationship Centres (FRC) and family dispute mediation plays a key role for improving outcomes and experiences arising from relationship breakdown in Australia[191]. They also provide vital opportunities for fathers who have interrupted contact with their children, to review those contact arrangements.

Unaddressed family violence issues

Family violence: The existence of past or current family violence within the relationship has a significant unspoken impact on all parties – the men, women and children. If non-resident fathers inappropriately attribute lack of the contact with their children to systemic issues potential family violence issues and its impacts are often not acknowledged. It is vital for all fathers to remain honourable, even in dishonourable situations and ensure that safety for all is their major intention and focus. See the Chapter 8 on generativity and family violence for more information.

Psychological factors

Grieving process: There is a direct connection between the intensity of the pre-separation father-child relationship and the outcome of the grieving process for non-resident fathers. Fathers with strong emotional attachment to their children before separation and divorce are more likely to experience the post-separation period as traumatic and are more likely to withdraw from parenting for a period of time. Often child disengagement relates to the level of pain experienced by the non-resident parent[192].

This was also found to be the case in Killeen and Lehmann's[193] study, during which one father said:

'Just not having daily input, not having the daily physical contact ... is hard'.

Mark filled with emotion, commented: 'It's very important ... he ah ... he's the first thing I think of probably ... of a morning ...' (referring to his five-year-old son) (p.15).

When separation occurs in families with young children, often there is little time for the development of father-child involvement routine. This may cause fathers an alarming sense of deprivation and exclusion from the child's life. Many fathers in this situation become anxious that the child will not know or remember them.

Child absence: Child absence can impact fathers' perception of their functioning as a parent post-separation. Feeling devalued as parents, fathers that may previously have been highly-involved and attached may describe themselves as being lost, having no structure in their lives, and generally anxious, helpless, and depressed[194]. These fathers may have spoken to few people about their feelings and the importance they attach to their fathering role. The crisis of separation can provide the first opportunity for this to be expressed.

Fathers' concerns for the child's safety in their absence: Many men have concerns about how they can protect their children and maintain their safety when they are no longer living with them. They become anxious when another man lives with the mother and the children. In some cases when another man is involved, this is seen as a direct threat to their role, bringing feelings of identity displacement and embarrassment. It is easy for this concern to be expressed as controlling behaviour towards the mother and children that has a very negative impact on all involved.

To deal with this, fathers need to recognise it is in his children's best interests for him to accept the new relationship. The expression 'the nearby guy' may be useful as it emphasises the relationship with the child, rather than 'the boyfriend' which focuses on the new adult relationship. The healthy development of all children relies on their easy access to connections with positive male role models. While 'the nearby guy' may not replace the biological father, he provides fathering responsibilities. When the father views and accepts their partner's new relationship from the child's viewpoint, they reduce the chance that their child will feel disloyal to their father if they accept this new man/partner in their family's life.

Role loss: Child absence is accompanied by role loss unless fathers can value the new and ongoing role they play in the children's lives. After separation, fathers can lose the identity and status they traditionally associated with being a 'dad'.

Alternatively, fathers need to acknowledge that post-separation fathering is not about reclaiming a role that still exists. Rather, it is important to acknowledge that the circumstances have changed. Consequently, the role would benefit from being restructured to suit the current needs of the children. However, there is no denying the fact that he is still the children's father, and this must be affirmed by significant people in his life.

The 'visiting' relationship: Disengaged fathers often view themselves as 'visiting' fathers, rather than legitimate carers of their child or children during the time they spend together. The constraint of the 'visiting' relationship is a significant component in the disengagement of those fathers who had an active role to play in their children's lives during the couple's relationship[195]. This is demonstrated by one father in the Killeen and Lehmann[196] study: *He lived in a caravan and felt this had an unfavourable effect on his contact, commenting: 'I feel inadequate because I'm not providing her with a room and that sort of stuff'* (p.15).

Being child-focused is an important skill for all fathers to develop. The man who says, 'just give me my kids and I will be okay' is not on a child-focused path. It is an expression of his needs and desires alone, rather than his response to what the child or children require. Post-separation, fathers have an opportunity to become more competent as parents, and be able to respond to the child's immediate needs. This is a challenge to which most men can rise, especially when they receive support from peers and practitioners. These fathers become valuable parents who are supportive and responsive to the child, providing a positive, non-pressured environment in which the children can relax and grow as themselves, rather than be exposed to high levels of conflict between parents.

Perceived effects of divorce on children: A primary factor associated with the disengagement of previously highly involved and attached fathers is their perception that their children are 'caught in the middle' of an ongoing conflict between parents. They may, therefore, choose to wait until the child is older before they attempted to re-establish contact.

The issue of conflict is reduced when both parents actively use strategies to avoid or deal with conflict in a child-supportive way. It is important for the fathers to acknowledge that separation impacts on all members of the family, but that ongoing conflict can have longer lasting ramifications for the children.

Parental Alienation: There are many degrees of parental alienation imposed upon many children when separation occurs. It can be shown by a lack of acknowledgement or respect by one parent for the other, their family and/or other people having direct influence on the child. An example of this might be stating a negative view of the other parent with regard to their feelings for the child, such as when a mother says, 'Your father doesn't love you, he doesn't even like you, and he didn't even want you'.

Alienation may also occur when one parent seeks to convince the child that the other parent is a threat to the child or the family. While these statements may contain some truth, some positive regard for the other parent relates directly to the child's own view of themselves. It is recognised by the authors that it is important for fathers to acknowledge that mutual respect between the parents would enhance relationships with their children.

The generative fathering framework as a tool to rebuild engagement

The generative fathering framework is a model for understanding the non-deficit approach to fathering, initially presented in the previous chapter. The generative approach mirrors the framework and skills of child-focused approaches in working with family separation. Child-focused practice occurs when professionals actively give the child a voice by helping the parent(s) to develop their understanding and awareness of their child's needs to encourage the parent(s) to keep this as a focus. A child-focused approach is commonly used in post-separation work to:

- Create an environment that supports disputing parents in actively considering the unique needs of each of their children.
- Facilitate a parenting agreement that preserves significant relationships and supports children's psychological adjustment to the separation, including recovery from parental acrimony and protection from further conflict.
- Support parents to leave the dispute resolution forum on higher rather than diminished ground with respect to their post-separation parenting.
- Ensure that the ongoing mediation/litigation process and the agreements or decisions reached reflect the basic psycho-developmental needs of each child, to the extent that they can be known without the involvement of the children.

Rebuilding a connection post-separation

The non-deficit perspective, an approach to understanding and working with fathers, suggests that most fathers are interested in family life and that their engagement with support services is influenced by a variety of relationship difficulties. These difficulties can compile and result in a phenomenon called '*generative chill*' that was initially introduced in Chapter 6. The challenge is how men can rebuild this generative connection. Professionals and close family members may desire to help men deal with the pain of their family separation, but it is the father's timing alone that will ultimately dictate when he is open to rebuilding connection, engagement or reunion with his child.

A dominant social view of separated fathers reflects images of their absence, disinterest, abandonment, disengagement, non-involvement, and how they can be labelled 'Disneyland Dads'. As the contact parent, they are often viewed as playing a secondary and less important role. Current research provides a different image which indicates that:

- fathers are generally important to their children's lives;
- continued contact with their father after separation enhances children's adjustment;
- fathers benefit from involvement with their children after separation; and
- fathers want to be involved with their children and to fulfil their responsibilities as a father[197,198].

Men's behaviour often reflects the attitude that 'good fathering means good providing'. The responsibility of providing for the family's needs influences men's level of self-esteem and the value they place on their family role. Hawkins and Dollahite's[199] research shows that unemployment can prompt working-class men to question their value to the family. Separated fathers are often more involved and active contributors of Child Support payments when they have a firm identity that is supported by other people around them. In the USA, Bryan[200] recognised that a father's unemployment and absence can result in problems of poverty, depression, violence and neglect for the mother and children left behind. Fathers, as represented in the wider community, generally undervalue how important their presence is to their children's schooling, gender identity, emotional stability, security and self-confidence.

The power of the birth story

Generativity is more easily harnessed when people respond usefully to an issue or someone that they perceive as more vulnerable than themselves. Most communities across the world recognise the inherent vulnerability of a baby. It is often at this important advent into parenthood that both parents, and particularly the father, review important life decisions. One easy way to enhance this narrative with men is for practitioners to ask the father to tell them about the birth story of one of their children. This is a very special opportunity because men usually allow the mother to tell the birth story (as they should).

However by telling their version fathers own their experience and the likely changes they face. The birth of a baby is so rich in vulnerability and the need for care that it increases the fathers' ability to connect and attach to the child. They become more conscious of their relationship to the child and the on-going role that they play.

Case study

> *An experienced family law mediator experimented in mediation sessions with the idea of asking both parents to talk about the birth of one of their children and telling each other about their memory. She initially thought clients would say, "You've got to be kidding." The opposite happened. Each parent launched into their story and the other parent started listening. This framed the mediation in a positive framework to begin with. It helps clients to be child and future-focused. It has made a significant change to a high-conflict process.*

Valuing differences in roles

Women are less likely to evaluate good mothering according to how well they provide for their children financially, or what they do in maintaining their relationship with their partner. Men, however, are more likely to evaluate their role in the family by using a limited range of criteria, for example, being the financial provider.

After separation occurs, fathers need to be able to define the new role they play in their children's lives. The use of educative groups for separated fathers aids the development of, and expression of new parenting roles. The new parenting role emphasises:

- that men can redefine their parenting relationship to highlight the unique opportunities that separated fathers experience;
- the unique and valuable qualities men play in their children's lives with ongoing involvement; and
- that the father is also the vital link to the paternal family of the child.

This new role can be poorly developed when fathers enter into a new relationship too quickly. Redefinition and co-parenting issues may not be adequately addressed, so confusion and disengagement are more likely. The new relationship may present a fresh start, even though it might conflict with a child-focused and child-supportive position. Acting as a block or defence for the father, it might interfere with the grieving process and reduce his ability to identify what impact the separation has had on himself and the child. This can result in a reduction of support for himself and towards his child, while relying on his new partner for relationship satisfaction.

Engaging separated fathers through the generativity framework

Generativity provides a strong framework to emphasise the role played by separated fathers regardless of the amount of time spent with their children. Generativity connections can be maximised by practitioners:

- Finding out the facts. How many children he has, their ages, when separation occurred, what orders are in place and when he last had contact with his children.
- Building a child focused connection as central to your relationship with him.
- Building on language that values respect, 'being a reasonable man', 'maintaining integrity', providing what your children need (emphasising safety, security and connection). Until proven otherwise, believe that the father has a shared interest in these values.
- Acknowledging and normalising feelings, particularly if the father sees himself being treated unfairly. Practitioners should reaffirm the importance of how fathers are seen today and the on-going role he plays in the present and future context.
- Building a strong metaphor of walking with him in the work you do. Find out how this may be helpful to him (using perceived equality) for guidance.
- Exploring what he can control in his situation, what he can influence and what he can't control or influence. Relate this to specific examples in his life.
- Affirming the importance of showing respect for the children's mother. Regardless of what has happened the children love her and will benefit from seeing this from their father. Explore the importance of timing – not being too impatient and also appreciating the positive aspects of what may already exist in times spent with his children.
- Supporting him to tune into the feelings and needs of his children and what is required to help make his life safe (abiding by any court orders), nurturing and valuing (towards key relationships in his life).
- Reflecting on past, present, and future reflections in life. When these three perspectives are reflected on simultaneous, it provides a generative lens where the present is impacted on by the past and the future relies on what happens now in the present.

- Encouraging him to keep a diary and live the values that are important to him and his children. If his friends have children, encourage him to maintain some interest and understand how quickly children develop and change.

This reflective story, from a case worker at a family relationship centre, has a strong theme of generativity:

During a psycho-educational group for fathers, I identified this man, Charlie (fictitious name), who seemed angry with his wife, Clare (fictitious name). Charlie was in the military. He had a young family and was separated from his wife. He spoke of Clare failing to understand the importance of his role in the military. He referred to the three young Australian soldiers killed last year in Afghanistan. He became righteous in his tone when he spoke of how they gave their life fighting for their country. Charlie demonstrated a strong sense of patriotism and camaraderie for his fallen countrymen. His conviction was strong. He explained that he, too, was going overseas and appeared quite proud of that fact.

As Charlie spoke of his relationship with Clare and their children, there seemed to be a disconnection from them. He spoke angrily of Clare, stating that she controlled when he saw the kids, ad said that she was "screwed up" and that she didn't understand the importance of his role. Clare was the target of his blame. I acknowledged the importance of his role in the military. I asked him what he meant by insisting that Clare didn't understand his role. He said she wanted him to "get out" and that was the source of much of their arguments. I suggested that it made him angry because Clare seemed to have misunderstood his intentions and the importance of his role in the family. He agreed.

I explored what was going on with Clare and Charlie. I suggested to Charlie that his wife might fear losing a husband and the father of her children by his serving in a combat zone. I asked if he had discussed her fears with her and found he hadn't. I directed the topic to loyalty and patriotism. I said the patriotism he had for his country was admirable but asked about his patriotism to his family. 'I'm not sure what you mean,' he replied. I explained that Clare was perhaps fearful of him being killed in combat and that this was very real for her as there were constant reminders on the television and internet and in newspapers. I added, 'You are very patriotic to your country, but there is also patrio-

tism, loyalty and honour owed to your family. They look at you to keep them safe and secure, and Clare is fearful if you're thousands of kilometres away in some foreign country with God knows what going on. Step into her shoes!' He didn't respond. Later I discussed the matter with my colleague to find out what he thought. We considered Charlie was an angry man and we felt we hadn't managed to get through to him. Charlie gave positive feedback in the evaluation form, but as for putting things into practice, we were doubtful.

A few weeks later, I was doing a telephone intake. As I spoke with the woman, she revealed that her co-parent had changed since coming to the centre. She reported a side she had never seen before in the several years they had been together. She told me he was not acting in anger and was spending more time with the children and with her. She told me they were even considering reconciliation. She said they were talking and discussing things really well. I looked down at the file and recognised the name. It was Clare. She was talking about Charlie. I asked her, 'So in all the years you have been together, have you ever seen him like this before?', 'No' she said. I asked her how she felt. She said she liked it and spoke of what a good man he had become. She said, "Before he would get very angry with me and the kids and yell, but now we talk!"

Engaging homeless men

When someone appears to have few traditional expressions of generativity in their life as they are alienated from their family, explore what connections they may inadvertently use on the streets. These connections are likely to centre on the care and support they provide to other peers or are found in their care of an important pet or animal. Generativity connections can be maximised by practitioners:

- Valuing the importance of the little choices they have in life i.e. where they sleep at night, which they trust.
- Finding out who they trust and are close to on the streets, at your centre and in their wider life. Safely discuss important relationships that have had or still are central in their life.
- Identifying what they have learned and continue to learn in those relationships.
- Building the metaphor of walking alongside them in the work you do. Find out how this may be helpful to them (use perceived equality)

for guidance.
- Asking how many children they have, their ages, what orders are in place and when they last had contact their children.
- Asking what is important about these relationships? What would they like to change about those relationships?
- Discussing what roles they identify they play amongst the people they hang-out with. What roles are important to them? If applicable discuss:
    1. Who or how do you protect others in your life?
    2. Who do you keep safe?
    3. What happens when the protection of others is misused?
    4. What is the difference between keeping someone safe and controlling them?
    5. When does protecting someone become abusive?
    6. How do you keep yourself safe?

Ways that men can deal with disengagement

The key for men to re-engage with their children is to recognise the significant pain involved in the disengagement process and redevelop the experience of *being-in-the-moment*[201] with their child/ren. While a strong emphasis is placed on the responsibilities men have after family separation has occurred, the word 'responsibility' has a wider meaning. Responsibility means 'response-ability'. Until proven otherwise, men and women have the ability to respond from a deeper place in their heart that focuses on their relationship with the child[202]. The recognition of the significance of the father-child relationship is the first step in nurturing positive responses.

The authors have found that most disengaged fathers hope that they will be able to regain the relationship connection with their children. Bryan[203] states, 'until he is able to do that, no matter how a man may try to deny it, he is divided' (p.19). Often after a period of disengagement, the possibility of reconnecting with their child/ren arises. Sometimes this emerges as a result of the men being around other people's children; they develop a deeper urge to reconnect with their own children.

To counter the men's belief that their children are better off if they have less involvement in their life, it is important for disengaged fathers to realise that their children may share many of the same feelings. When the initial attempt to reconnect occurs, both the father and the children can share similar feelings. They both have a fantasy about the reunion after not seeing each other for a significant period of time as well as a sense of loss and bewilderment about the separation and a possible wish for a workable route back into each other's life[204].

The reconnection of fathers with their children should always focus on the safety and well-being of the child. Neither the mother nor the father should be with their children if their behaviour is in any way detrimental to the child.

Through the operation of a fathers' centre, the authors have observed that fathers experience this disengagement pain as 'haunting' when reminded of their children. When men are asked if they have children, they may respond in a less than positive manner, such as, 'Well you might say that, I don't get to see them'. This will be the end of a dialogue started with positive intention, and will most likely not be revisited. Fathers would benefit if guided to a more positive response, such as 'Yes, I have two great kids and they live with their mum'. Similarly, the 'haunting'[205] can occur when fathers report being around other children – hearing them call to their dads can be an upsetting reminder of their loss. The father can maintain the love he feels for his own children through contact he has with other children, thus developing an appreciation that fathers, and other significant men, are important in children's lives.

Fathers who have rebuilt engagement with their children have identified a number of useful steps:

1. Maintain a journal over several months that enables the men to prepare themselves emotionally for reunion with their children. It is useful to develop an emotional map that recounts key memories of the child/ren and then over time focuses on the development of a clear picture of where their child is today and what their life is like. It is also useful for the father to create a narrative time line of their life, a life history in their own words, as this will help when communication starts with his children.

2. It is important for the men to obtain current information about their child/ren, if they have not already done so. School reports and current photographs and contact with the school will be useful. This will focus the father on the present context and replace images of the past. The unique and valuable qualities the children possess must be acknowledged by the father as this will be important in dialogue with the children to build their self-esteem.

3. Negative ways of responding to issues can be addressed by writing a list of positive strengths about themselves. It may also be useful to create a gratitude list of fifty things they are grateful about in their life (present and past). The fact that their children are healthy, cared for and safe should be high on the list as this will support the appreciation for the mother's role.

4. Identify a professional support person or mentor. Often professionals can coach and support men in this process as they share their new learning. It is important for the men to develop useful strategies for dealing with their emotions, such as talking to someone, exercising, cleaning, walking, etc. They need to manage their health and take care of themselves.

5. Access to a mediation service may be useful in contacting the mother if communication is difficult. A skilled mediator can be a vital resource in these situations. A mediator or legal representative will be important if there is any order restricting direct contact. In any case, the father should seek legal advice from a Family Law Specialist Solicitor/ Lawyer about their intended actions.

6. Humility and responsibility are core values that will support the reconnection process. Writing a list of the key lessons they have learnt through their life is one of the exercises that can assist fathers to develop the necessary emotional flexibility to deal with the experience of reuniting with their child. It is useful for fathers to join a support group for separated fathers to reinforce the use of a new business-like relationship with the mother[206]. This business-like relationship with the mother of their children has been reported to be vital by fathers who have shared care responsibilities because it assists in disentangling the adult relationship from the parenting relationship[207].

7. It is important for the fathers to prepare for the reunion with their children slowly, without having firm expectations of what will occur. It is useful for them to lighten up and value the good things currently happening in their life. Fathers need to be careful about making promises to their child/ren or the mother that they may not be able to keep.

8. It is important for men to be able to show positive regard for the child's mother, as re-establishing the relationship with the child does not take place in isolation, and requires them to avoid or manage any negative communication and conflict that may arise.

Concluding thoughts on generativity among separated fathers

This chapter explored why contact between separated fathers and their children can break down and lead to disengagement. In summary, there are many factors that result in fathers disengaging from their children, such as increased geographic distance between a father and child\ren; increased economic demands; father-child alienation; new family responsibilities; conflict with the mother of their children and their inability to deal with either their own anger or the mother's anger.

While many fathers may find it difficult to express their feelings in words, the primary motivator in their lives is often relationships, especially the relationship with their children. From the child's perspective, every child has a biological father whether he is present, absent or even deceased. They have a natural curiosity about their father because it leads to answers about who they are themselves and why they look, feel, think and behave as they do. Children need many different sources of familial input to understand and value their own existence. Positive support for the father-child relationship is as healthy and vital for children as it is for the father.

However, this is only true for the father who is willing to be open to the changes that separation creates and who is willing to seek new knowledge and the support required to meet the new challenges. The post-separation experience is not about 'getting even' with or seeking revenge on the mother, but involves the subtle nurturing of a stronger relationship with their children. When this focus is achieved, many fathers report that after separation they achieve a new, deeper and more meaningful relationship with their children. Often the relationship is both richer and stronger than before the separation occurred in spite of the confusion in role experienced by many fathers today.

After contact has broken down, separated fathers are likely to re-involve themselves with their children when they receive respectful support that nurtures the significance of the father-child relationship. Professional support needs to be accessible, easy to understand, relevant to their immediate situation, of high quality, and yet still affordable.

Practitioners need to use a variety of theoretical approaches to understand child protection issues due to the complexity and variation of issues experienced. A key theory for understanding the motivations, actions and responses used by many men is best captured by the generative perspective. Reviewing men's behaviour through generative care and not the other common traditional roles such as being a breadwinner, a companion, a moral guide, a protector, a disciplinarian and a co-parent, provides a strengths-based and child focussed approach to working with men.

The generative perspective supports the definition of 'social fathering' as a key point for engaging and working alongside a wider range of men in the child's life. Adopting a social view of fathering is important not only because the term is inclusive, but because its use implies recognition of the diversity of roles men as fathers play in the lives of children in contemporary families today (Sullivan & Howard 2000). The more men are responsive to their child's needs, the more they will be involved in social expressions of generative care within their local community. This chapter has attempted through the linking of some current local research with practice to address the complex issue of working with men as fathers.

Since contemporary fathering specifically is increasingly diverse and more complex than it was three decades ago, family based and community services would benefit greatly by focussing on father presence and its benefit. In particular, there is a further need for practice-based research into successful interventions with fathers such as the one described in this chapter, in particular men who have perpetrated family violence and are still involved with their family.

CHAPTER 7:

GENERATIVITY AND FATHERING CHILD/REN WITH SPECIAL NEEDS

Often the birth of a child with special needs is an experience that all parents have least preparation. Both parents are thrown into survival mode as they struggle to obtain a clear diagnosis for their child's situation, cope with the many unknowns and find their best response. For many mothers, the early intervention process is framed around the immediate care that includes continual involvement with the child. For the father, many men cope by supporting the mother and ensuring that the family has the resources that are required. Both the general community services sector and disability programs recognise that the best interests of the child are served by both parents being actively involved in the child's life[208]. However in practice, it is the primarily the mother who is present when professional supports are available to the child.

Many families ultimately experience separation and/or divorce before the child turns 18 years old due to increased pressure on families when supporting children with special needs. Yet, when fathers are actively involved in their children's life, the children are more likely to have stronger coping and adaptation skills, better problem solving skills, stay in school longer, achieve better at school, have longer lasting relationships, higher work productivity, better self-esteem and better control of actions. The benefits also flow on to the men as engaged fathers are more likely to have better overall health, higher self-esteem, more positive self-image and greater work satisfaction[209].

When a child has special needs, the father's experience of generativity may also be challenged. Their expectations of parenthood and what will be required have been significantly disrupted. It is important for fathers to deepen their generative connection by being engaged as an active agent in the care of and support of both the mother and the children. It is important that fathers are involved with support services and actively make choices about how they think, feel, believe and act rather than only reacting to events outside their control. They need to rework their responses and take action that flows from their desires and commitments to care for their child with special needs[210].

Issues identified by fathers regarding parenting children with special needs include: feelings of self-blame; denial of the extent of disability; effects on the marriage; uncertainty over the diagnosis; constant strain of caring; benefits of meeting other families in similar situations; restrictions on family life; difficulty telling other people about the disability; feeling guilty about having negative feelings about their child; negative experiences of service provision; and dealing with negative reactions in the community[211].

Understanding the emotional world of men as fathers is integral. The reflection below, highlights what many fathers with a child with special needs think about as parents, but rarely express to other people:

"The single greatest challenge I faced as a father to a child with a disability was trying to accept the reality that I cannot "fix" the "problem". All parents wish to shield their children from all harm in the world, but parents (and particularly fathers) feel like they have 'failed' to live up to this. The feeling is: 'Not only does my child have a disability, but I'm useless, helpless because I could not stop it and now I can't do anything to fix it either'. There was nothing more painful in my life than watching my child have seizures in my arms and being completely helpless to do anything at all about them. It was not until I had professional counselling that I could focus on something other than blaming myself and acknowledge that my daughter wasn't blaming me either, nor holding it against me, that these things were happening to her".

Research suggests that fathers report a range of concerns when supporting a child with special needs. For example, one study asked 48 dads of children with chronic illnesses to complete the Family Perception Inventory and identify concerns they had. These included the child's health (98% identified this as a concern), feeling worn out (73%), doing enough family activities together (96%), making the family comfortable and happy (94%), the responsibility of caring for the family (81%), extra demands on time (88%), sexual relationship with spouse (87%), having enough fun and relaxation (85%), and enough time alone with spouse (83%)[212]. These additional concerns have been found to be linked to elevated levels of stress among mothers and fathers of children with special needs, compared to the parents of children without special needs [213]. As a result, stress management and a focus on building stronger parental communication should be addressed within therapy programs. Programs need to be tailored to meet the needs of both fathers and mothers[214].

Further, research suggests that interventions specifically involving fathers in programs have important flow on effects to the support of the rest of the family. A study of 60 sets of parents of a child with severe intellectual disability assessed the extent of father involvement in the lives of their child, and both parents' satisfaction with this involvement. Findings showed that fathers are most involved in playing, nurturing, discipline and deciding on services. Most mothers were satisfied with the extent of father's help, with higher levels of satisfaction being associated with higher marital adjustment and lower child-rearing burden. This study concludes the importance of including fathers in programs for families of children with special needs[215].

Challenges and barriers to the involvement of fathers in programs for the families of children with special needs

Research indicates that there are several barriers for fathers in accessing services to support families caring for children with special needs. Some prominent barriers include:

- fathers may often acknowledge less to others that they have a child with special needs;
- fathers may minimise the idea that support is needed and not wanting others prying into their life;
- fathers may focus on work and other commitments;
- fathers may attribute less priority is given to accessing support group;
- fathers may believe that primary care is the mother's role;
- professionals not knowing how to approach fathers when they do access services; and
- if fathers do want to access services, meetings may be held at times they are unable to attend due to work or other commitments.

When your program provides home visits for families of children with special needs

Programs need to allow fathers a degree of flexibility and choice, and venues which are non-threatening and culturally neutral. Programs or meetings need to be offered on days when the fathers may not work or in the evenings or on weekends to allow as many of them to attend as possible. It is critical to build initial engagement with the fathers before you invite them to attend the first session. This process enables them to clarify questions and build a connection with the practitioner. If the fathers is at work, practitioners can telephone within them within 48 hours of the visit to provide some feedback, observations and ask if they have any questions.

When your program provides group meetings for families of children with special needs

Successful groups have the following features:
- a positive group climate stressing the strengths of children;
- focus on what can be accomplished, rather than obstacles;
- the group meets the needs of members, whether that be emotional support, information, education and/or advocacy; and
- require practitioner s who motivate/organise and provide contacts[216].

In promoting your group meetings, it is the experience of the authors that 70% of the fathers require having some form of phone contact with the facilitators as a pre-requisite for them to attend the first session. This process enables them to clarify questions and build a connection with the staff.

It is important to portray a welcoming impression with staff:
- ringing all the participants and speak to them individually before the program commences (very important);
- meeting new members before the meeting especially when families have a high level of needs;
- providing details about transport, parking;
- welcoming new fathers, find out what they would like from the group, explaining what will happen in the meeting and introducing the new members to other members;
- arranging seats in a circle;
- allowing time for talking and listening to each other;
- avoiding the use of jargon and don't refer to people without explaining who they are; and

- remembering and using people's names.

Groups need members who will share in the workload of the group. For example:

- everyone should help decide on the group's activities;
- members views should be heard;
- members should identify roles or activities they are happy to help with;
- rotate jobs regularly and involve new members;;
- sharing information and making use of people's networks is important;
- give everyone a chance to contribute where their skills lie; and
- do not let older members dominate[217].

Using generative questions

Useful generative questions include[218]:

1. What challenges make it difficult for you to choose to meet your child/ren's needs?
2. How have you made choices with your partner that address the tough dilemmas you face in meeting your needs and those of your child/ren?
3. If you were to take action right now that would benefit your child/ren, what would it be?
4. What is your greatest strength in meeting your child/ren's needs as a family?
5. May I join you in a search for strengths in your family that you can develop to contribute better to your child/ren's development?
6. If you could build on one of your strengths to benefit your children, what would it be?
7. What do you gain from your child/ren's resilience (strength to stand in their challenges)?
8. What sacrifices could you make now to give to your children that they need most?
9. What values are most important for you to pass along to others and your children?
10. What commitments for your child's future have you made in the past that are being challenged now?
11. How do you draw on others in the community to help maintain your generative connections?

CHAPTER 8:

GENERATIVE APPROACH AND DOMESTIC VIOLENCE

At a time where social awareness regarding the impact of domestic violence is on the increase, it is important to that remember most fathers do not use domestic violence in their intimate relationships. It is equally important to remember that all men can actively take a stand against violence by reflecting on our own relationships, being an active bystander, and challenging the permissive assumptions that indirectly support gendered violence across all communities.

The generative framework can be used to increase insight among men and reduce the use of family violence by highlighting the tension between the desire to be a good father and the threat of the fathers' violent actions. Over the past few decades this tension has been highlighted as a part of effective media campaigns (i.e. the Freedom from Fear Campaign) and also provides a discussion framework to deepen discussion about domestic violence with men. This chapter highlights several examples of how these forces can be utilised in practice.

The Freedom from Fear Campaign

In 1995 the Western Australian government's Family and Domestic Violence Taskforce developed an innovative non-punitive campaign called Freedom from Fear as a part of the governments' long term strategic framework to reduce family and domestic violence[219]. The campaign primarily focused on men who have used violence (or showed potential to use it), asking them to seek help to change their violent ways[220]. The logic behind Freedom from Fear was that if violent men voluntarily changed their violent behaviour it would not only reduce the incidence of violence, but also reduce the fear felt by their female partners and children. After extensive interview testing among men who use family violence, they chose to use a child-focused approach that explored the impact of family violence and supported men to access local behaviour change services. In 2008 this initiative was successfully replicated at Hull in the United Kingdom.

The initial task force used focus groups and individual interviews to develop the most effective approach to reduce incidence of family and domestic violence[221]. They found that the theme of criminal sanctions, community intervention and social disapproval had little impact in the testing stage. The theme of *damage to partner* was not seen as a key motivation by men who had used violence. This theme was dismissed as likely to be ineffective. However, in contrast, the *effect on and damage to children* was universally seen as a very powerful notion among men who had used violence:

All fathers in the pilot group expressed strong feelings for their kids (while very few expressed any feelings of fondness for their partners).

Their children's reactions to specific instances of domestic violence had a very vivid impact on many men in the pilot groups who had used violence.

Many of the younger men who had used violence could relate to their own feelings when they were kids, and some talked about how domestic violence had affected them as children. Thus, this theme had relevance whether or not they themselves had children.

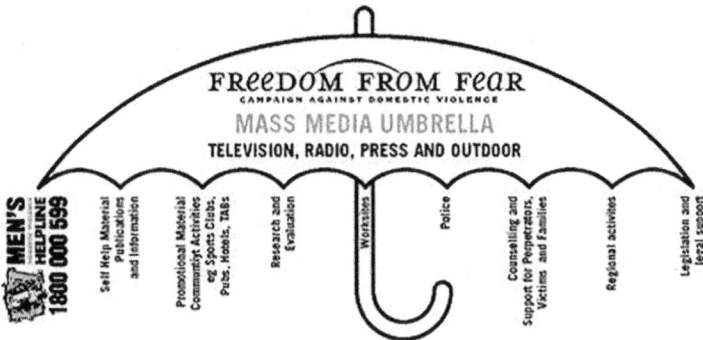

Figure 4: Overview of Freedom from Fear Campaign

Consequently, the development of family and domestic violence interventions that focus on violent men's role as fathers shows significant promise as a viable intervention tool. Usually fathers are viewed as rigid and authoritative[222], uninvolved in their children's lives and negligent of their basic needs (including those thwarted by the violence). A more complex picture of violent men as fathers was portrayed by Fox and her colleagues[223]. This qualitative study focused on the fathering of eight men who participated in Men's Behaviour Change (MBC) groups and found that the men expressed feelings of guilt, shame, remorse and responsibility regarding the damage they caused as fathers and they wished to fix it. The men's fathering role contributes significantly to their sense of self, which in turn may lead to a less defensive inspection of their abusive behaviours and an increased motivation to access further support. Below are the images used in the Freedom from Fear campaign in Hull, England[224].

Figure 5: Images from the UK Freedom from Fear campaign

Focusing on the tension of generativity

It is a cornerstone of men's behaviour-change frameworks to not work with men who use violence if the harm they have inflicted on their partners and children remains unacknowledged. Men who use domestic violence are simultaneously vulnerable and harmful. Best practice centres on supporting men to recognize their privilege, responsibility and their own ethical responses to their violence. To hold this tension, focus on how positive attitudes lay at the core of the men's perceptions of fathering in general and of their own fathering while acknowledging the violence, its consequences and the choices that exist. In using this perspective, fathering is one of the most important domains of life, if not the most important, which includes men viewing themselves as good fathers. This is a significant motivation of behaviour change and is already used in a variety of men's behaviour change programs[225].

There is often an unspoken tension in many men between the **yearning** to be a good dad and the individual **challenge**, and the impact this has on their children:

- To "live for your child".
- To "give your kids everything and be the best possible dad".
- To "be a good dad"

and the tension of:

- Exposing the children to violence
- How family violence impacts on their children
- Being the controller
- Being an absent dad

Overall, the men who use domestic violence often present themselves as good fathers and minimise the impact that the violence has on their children. Perel and Peled[226] conducted many men's behaviour change interviews and noticed various ways the men used to construct their image as good fathers. These included providing material needs, protection, education and creating a warm connection with the children. In the spirit of traditional conceptions of fathering, the breadwinner or provider roles took precedence over the other attributes of good fathering. When using generativity, this hope and aspiration is acknowledged, along with the fear or challenge that the threat of violence creates. They regularly found fathers expressed strong reactions towards the impact violence had on their children. The aim of generative discussions is to link the significance of past/present/future reflections that acknowledge these tensions that, unanimously, leave fathers with a strong yearning for connection with their children and an understanding that their violence is a significant threat:

'I was less than a good father. I would call it a bad father, because it passes on a kind of trauma to the child.' (Freedom from Fear MBC group)

'All the blows, he saw all these things, all the shouting, all the quarrels, all these not nice things. He absorbed it. Listen, this child is already soaked to the skin, excuse me, in this shit, and it's not appropriate.' (Freedom from Fear MBC group)

'I think if you saw your children cowering or hiding, or even flinching from you, because they thought you were going to hit them, I think that would be a really big wakeup call... certainly more so than [if you saw] your wife or partner cowering in a corner.' (Freedom from Fear general public focus group)

'It petrified me as a child, and the one thing I don't want to do is make my child see me as a monster... I have shouted at my wife and I've seen the look on my son's face.' (Freedom from Fear BME focus group)

'And that, that will stay with me forever... just that look on his face. A mixture of disgust and terror, and I think just the fact that a 12-year-old saw what I was doing was just probably the hardest thing to bear.' (Freedom from Fear MBC group)

The yearning for a close and warm relationship with the children was displayed in many of the interviews. This yearning, often unattainable, played a central role in the drama of the interviewees' fathering. The drama was intensified by the clash between the men's image of 'the good father' who maintained a warm relationship with his children and the processes of tension as described above.

The key steps in working the generative tensions:

What is a key relationship that has greater vulnerability than himself?

Focus on significant hopes and dreams for that relationship

Discuss the fears and anxieties for that relationship. Name the threats.

Focus on important issues using relevance, faith building and honesty/directness.

Discuss what choices exist that enable him to strengthen this key generative connection.

The findings presented by Perel and Peled's[227] tell the fathering story of men who were violent towards their partners. The men's basic attitude to fathering was positive. Fathering was perceived as being of the utmost importance, and the men devoted considerable efforts to being a 'good father' as they perceived it. They felt they were indeed good fathers. Their aspirations, however, were undermined by internal and external forces that included:

- Their own childhoods
- Their personal limitations
- The children's exposure to violence
- The experience of co-parenting

The violence sets off a process of constriction, accompanied by feelings of frustration and yearning, through the father's controlling and violent presence in the home by accelerating separation, divorce or disconnection from the home, and by further damaging the adult relationship. The quality of the adult relationship is a major factor affecting the quality of fathering. Fathers tend to withdraw from their children when in conflict with the mother.

Implementing a child-focused approach

Bring children's stories into the program – their experiences of family violence and how it affects them. Bring and use the adult's reflections as a child.

- Use perspectives of being a child/parent.
- Pose the question, "How would you feel as a child watching family violence occur between your parents?"
- Explore reflections of their childhood – ask the men to write a letter to their fathers; use discussion about what they missed from their fathers and what they would like as fathers/future fathers.
- Promote empathy building – that the child's needs are greater and more vulnerable than their own.
- Focus on men's strengths, their love for their children.
- Set up activities groups for fathers and children.
- Use positive images that are displayed on the fridge.
- Ask, "Will your child be able to come to you in the hard and difficult times?"

Building cooperation with men

- Establish confidentiality.
- Create a safe environment (for individuals and the group).
- Support the development of trust.
- Use direct language.
- Use homework to encourage integration with the rest of their life.
- Avoid asking about feelings; use the sharing of stories and "What impact did that have?"
- Reframe old patterns or behaviours and look for exceptions.
- Use goal and boundary setting.
- Encourage accountability and ownership of the change process.
- Encourage responsibility – use solution-focused approaches.
- Encourage transparency – it reduces suspicion.
- Refer the men to a behaviour change group.
- Give permission for men to be honest.
- Engage the men regarding issues, and brainstorm their ideas.
- Develop new tools to deal with their anger by being more empathic and assertive.

CHAPTER 9:

GENERATIVITY AND CULTURALLY DIVERSE FATHERS

Working with culturally diverse fathers

As identified in previous chapters, generativity is expressed through developmental, relational, spiritual, and ethical dimensions. This is equally true across different cultural contexts. Generativity values a culture's strengths and opportunities along with the challenge to support and care for others in society instead of self-interest.

An effective position for community service/health workers when working cross-culturally, and especially with fathers from culturally diverse backgrounds, is to adopt a 'safe uncertainty' approach. This approach attributes equal value to professional expertise and the knowledge and expertise of the client, with regard to their unique situation. It has been described as being in the state of 'informed not-knowing'[228]. That is, practitioners are never the 'expert', 'right' or in full possession of 'the truth'. A key focus of this approach is to seek understanding rather simply acquire knowledge of the client's situation. When practitioners are more informed about the life experiences of people from culturally diverse communities, they can become aware of their own cultural biases and then recognise and harness the cultural narratives of the 'other' in a truly strengths-based practice.

A significant component of the engagement process with culturally diverse fathers is for the worker to consider:

- The key issues experienced by the client.
- The underlying impacts of that experience.
- The associated challenges experienced when addressing these issues.

Practitioners need to be genuinely interested in finding out about the background and experiences of the fathers, and the meaning they attached to those experiences. The extent of how far a worker goes into the client's past depends on the context and nature of the work. The most important message is that practitioners should adopt an inquiring mindset that is guided by genuine interest in knowing about the client's situation from their point of view. This becomes the medium for drawing out the narrative, providing invaluable validation and normalising the clients' response to their experiences.

When fathers from culturally diverse backgrounds come to see a practitioner they believe that the worker has some expertise that will help alleviate their problem. Practitioners are more effective when they have already developed some knowledge about their client's culture and gender by engaging in dialogue with colleagues and friends; attending cultural awareness training; watching documentaries; reading books, etc.

Practitioners are more effective if they have explored, through professional supervision or training, their own socialisation experience and attitudes to achieving culturally sensitive practice. It is useful for them to appreciate how men and women live generativity in that culture and the assumed values that support this. Practitioners hear the client's story with some knowledge about their background, but not with full possession of 'the truth'. If practitioners become as informed as possible about themselves and those they perceive as different, they will be able to listen in a way that takes into account cultural biases. In the case of refugee fathers, it is important to consider the overlap and complex interaction between issues associated with the aftermath of traumatic experiences in the context of organised violence, the problems related to the exile, migration and resettlement processes, and the trials and difficulties that are part and parcel of the normal life cycle[229].

Many of the refugee fathers who come to Australia experience a significant role change. Through these changes, refugee fathers (like many other fathers) have few opportunities to talk through their concerns with someone else. These changes often threaten their sense of generativity, even though they respond to issues in the best way they can. Their aspiration to protect their family has to be redefined in Australia because it may have a very different expression than what was culturally appropriate in their country of origin. The new context involves changing thoughts about:

- Viewing themselves with honour for being the father or patriarch of their family.

- Identifying who they are in their community and the role they play in the family.
- Revaluing the meaning of their prestige, status and dignity in the family and community.
- Being the main income earner.
- Providing external protection to other family members and keeping them safe.
- Having a clear purpose and role in the family/community.

It is important to talk through the roles and expectations they held before coming to Australia and how these have changed. Redefine the changes as a new chapter in their life for what generativity may now mean. Encourage them to remain up-to-date with changes in their country of origin because the sociocultural environment that existed when they left it is often concretised as the normal and ideal set of community values for many years into the future. An example of this is that the attitudes towards women and their freedom in the community may have recently changed in their country of origin. However, people often idealise the values that existed at the time they left as a refugee. Another example is around dress code. This is especially relevant to those families that practice the wearing of hijab. It is important to discuss expectation around these issues.

> *Laila is a 16 year old from a CALD background. She lived with her family in a popular neighbourhood in Melbourne. Since Laila turned 13, she has been having difficulties with convincing her father to participate in a dance group at her high school. The father too has been having difficulties in convincing Laila to wear the hijab. From the father's perspective, he has to do all he can to protect the cultural and religious heritage of Laila. His love for Laila makes him want to protect her from losing her culture and heritage. On the other hand, Laila is frustrated by her father's behaviour. She sees her father as controlling and never in her interest, while her father sees her as a challenging daughter who doesn't want to uphold their cultural and religious heritage.*

Generativity in this situation recognises the value of traditional norms whilst the father recognising that his daughter's needs in this new country are also a central consideration. The question can be framed as how can the father's protectiveness be used to support his daughter the best way he can. This is only achieved through negotiation with the daughter along with teamwork by the family around her.

Important considerations when working with culturally diverse fathers:

- **Consider the impact of the past experience of their migration to Australia.** Many culturally diverse fathers, whether they are refugees or from refugee-like backgrounds, have experienced some forms of difficulty in their country of origin and migration process. Coming to Australia creates a great sense of hope and the expectation of a better life for themselves and their families. These expectations are not always achieved due to challenges of resettlement in a new country. The impact of unmet expectations can lead to unexplained frustrations, anger and a sense of hopelessness.

- **Work towards building the client's sense of control and safety, and their meaning and purpose in life.** Help them re-establish their dignity and value [and] reconnect them to wider society[230]. Adopt a curious openness that helps you to understand the client's situation. Be person-centred, but don't probe too much. Show interest and positive regard for them and their background. Be mindful of triggers and the impact of past trauma issues when setting and communicating your role and service. Be transparent and honest, familiarising the client with aspects of confidentiality and privacy, and being upfront about your role.

- **Be aware of how easily the client can be overwhelmed.** Many newly arrived culturally diverse families easily become overwhelmed by the processes and stresses that settling into a new country involves. At times, a father is quite likely to have a smaller set of relationships or networks to talk through these changes and may appear more isolated or frustrated. Sometimes it may be difficult for parents to provide for basic parenting responsibilities due to the pressures or stress involved. Many of these pressures and stresses on the father centre on obtaining new employment, a change in his potential job role due to a lack of recognition of his original qualification, concern about the future, child/family needs, and worries about overseas issues and responsibilities in his country of origin.

- **Create opportunities to talk about the role changes that have occurred.** The fathers have experienced significant cultural change around ideas and expectations of how their family operates. This includes gender relations, individualism versus collectivism, and extended family contexts versus nuclear families. They may need to learn new skills, such as cooking for the family, because the mother is likely to obtain employment in some situations. This is a new role that may be trivialised by other fathers from their community as it challenges traditional expectations and masculinities, and is seen as a woman's responsibility. Refer to Appendix B for a sculpture exercise to explore role change.

- **Value that the father loves and cares for his children.** Newly arrived culturally diverse families have often undertaken flight or migration in the hope of improving future prospects for their children. Discuss the care of their children:
  - How is this achieved in Australia?
  - How do they keep their family safe?
  - What is the difference between keeping someone safe and controlling them, or when does it become abusive?
  - How do they balance and provide for what their children need?
- **Support the CALD father's development of new Education/ information; Communication; Flexibility family-based skills.** Provide opportunities for fathers to develop conceptual understanding children's need for autonomy and independence as important factors for success in their new country of settlement. However, care should be taken not to impose a strict definition of autonomy that pushes the idea of distancing oneself from others. One of the greatest sources of tensions CALD fathers have to deal with is the divide between the collectivist and the individualistic approach to family.
- **Engage with CALD fathers through:**
  - **Process and outcome** – CALD clients engage best when the process is purposeful, meaningful with positive experience. Consider the process as important as the outcome.
  - **Beginning with known to unknown** – CALD clients like all adults, respond effectively to modes of engagement that draw on their prior life experience or what they know before building on the new idea of what to be known.
  - **Ability to smoothly facilitate a way out of contrasting ideas and concepts-** Effective engagement with CALD client also requires the staff/worker to be competent in facilitating discussion on controversial topics and contrasting ideas.

It is worth stating again that working with culturally diverse fathers is like working with any other fathers. Don't feel that your skills are insufficient or that you are facing an "exotic" situation beyond your knowledge. The biggest difference is that you have to learn more about their specific past experiences and the impact the experiences may have on their personal situations. Also, practitioners need a developed sense of self-awareness and self-knowledge with particular focus on understanding their own cultural biases.

Generative factors leading towards a successful cultural transition

1. Open mindedness - Open-mindedness is demonstrated by a willingness to try to understand and appreciate (although not necessarily to adopt) the values and beliefs of others and the fact that a different point of view is equally valid.
2. Sense of humour - A sense of humour is important because in another culture there are many things that lead one to cry, get angry, or be annoyed, embarrassed, or discouraged. The ability to laugh it off and not take one's self or the situation too seriously will help guard against sadness.
3. Ability to cope with failure - The ability to tolerate failure is critical because everyone fails at something when they enter a completely new cultural environment. Persons who go overseas are often those who have been successful in their home environments and thus may have rarely experienced failure. Experience with failure is important in developing a range of coping behaviours.
4. Communicativeness - Many situations in other cultures are confusing and ambiguous. A person who wants to adapt as smoothly as possible needs to be able to express his/her feelings and thoughts, as well as to be able to ask for help in interpreting unfamiliar behaviours and subtle cultural cues.
5. Flexibility and adaptability - The ability to respond to or to tolerate the ambiguity of new situations is a crucial factor in cross-cultural adjustment. This may mean having to alter and/or give up familiar behaviour patterns and become familiar with or take on new behaviours of the new culture.
6. Curiosity - Curiosity is the demonstrated desire to know about other people, places, ideas, etc. This skill is important for people settling in a new country because they are constantly being confronted with new and different events and behaviours, and a genuine interest in those differences usually leads to positive response.

7. Positive and realistic expectations - It is important for recent arrivals in a new country to know that even though there may be great expectations about what the new country will bring, it is also a process that is often difficult and at times overwhelming. There can be intense emotional ups and downs as the person goes through a range of emotions from very positive to very negative as they adjust to their new lives, but that if they persevere through the challenges the rewards will be reaped.

8. Tolerance for differences - A person will need to be able to tolerate people who have different values, beliefs, and practices. This implies an inner strength to be able not only to learn about others, but also to feel secure within one's self while in the company of others who may feel, look, and act in a different manner.

9. Positive regard for others - This factor includes the ability to express warmth, empathy, respect, and positive regard for other people. People are most effective when they are able to communicate this positive regard for others, even when a situation or behaviour may make them feel uncomfortable.

10. Sense of self - A clear, secure feeling about oneself is usually present in individuals who are neither weak nor overbearing in their relationships with others. Persons with this strong, secure sense of themselves stand up for what they believe but do not cling to those beliefs in the face of new information.

Working with Aboriginal and Torres Strait Islander fathers

To many Aboriginal men, fathering is the most important and challenging commitment in their lives. Prior to colonisation, Aboriginal people were hunters and gatherers. After colonisation, that identity was gradually eroded in urban Aboriginal people. And yet it is still part of their nature and in their blood. There is still, for some men, a sense of hopelessness, loss and lack of self-esteem. This may not be the case in remote communities where people still live traditionally. But even there, they still have their own unique community challenges.

When working with Aboriginal men, the main thing you need to do is to build up that self-esteem; in a sense, to get that hunting and gathering role back within them. This today means earning a wage, providing for their family and caring for their family. That's what has been lost and why many Indigenous people are in so much trouble today. In many Aboriginal communities, many of the leaders are outspoken women. The Aboriginal men sit back and don't project themselves well. This is now slowly starting to change with the development of Aboriginal men's groups. There is a new excitement and expectation through the work of people in organisations that are working with men. The men are starting to get back their self-esteem, sense of belonging and sense of pride.

The messages for Aboriginal fathers are no different to the messages all fathers need to remember. However, they are more critical and essential for Aboriginal communities due to the social history they have experienced. The following messages need to be reinforced in fliers, resources, programs and chats you have with Aboriginal dads (SNAICC & FAC, 2013):

- **Be there.** Make time with your kids, enjoy just being with them, laughing with them, playing with them and showing them your feelings and love.
- **Be proud.** Respect and be proud of your culture, and let the kids be proud of you.
- **Protect.** Be child-centred, making good decisions for the best interests of your children. Think about how you talk, act and care for them so they grow up safe, happy and proud.
- **Connect.** Be involved with your children at the start and all through their life. Mistakes and challenges will occur, but keep the connection going by letting them know you are there for them.
- **Talk and listen** to your children. Also talk with your kids and to other dads about what it is like being a dad.
- **Feel good.** Mistakes and challenges will occur, but enjoy your kids and enjoy being a dad.
- **The journey.** Think about the lessons you have learnt about life and tell your children and grandchildren about them.

NEXT STEPS...

This book has highlighted that there are a range of strategies practitioners can use to engage men as fathers (if safe to do so) using the Generative Fathering Framework. This has important implications for researchers and professionals. Opening up new ways of seeing men as fathers beyond the heavily infused notions of risk and danger can assist professionals to look deeper into the basis of father's identity as men and as parents. This book has sought to provide an alternative perspective and to help professionals keep fathers in mind in their work, raising awareness, and encouraging their presence.

There needs to be a greater focus involving men as clients in the community services sector. Since contemporary fathering specifically is increasingly diverse and more complex than it was three decades ago, the Australian community service profession would benefit greatly from the funding of practice-based research. In particular, there is a greater need for practice-based research into successful interventions with fathers that are often are described as vulnerable or hard to reach as well as male caregivers who have perpetrated family violence and are still involved with families. So far in Australia to date, there have been gaps in this type of research leaving professionals without evidence-based practice frameworks to draw upon in their work. In terms of future research directions, it would be beneficial for professionals to apply the generativity concepts to their practice with fathers and evaluate the results.

It is important to encourage fathers to develop strong attachments with their children as it will benefit not only the child but also the mother, the father and their relationship and their connection to society in general.

Generativity is a life force that informs best practice in supporting strong parental attachments, being a carer, dealing with disabilities and drug and alcohol issues. Practitioners can use generativity as a framework that deepens father-child engagement and connections. This strengths-based framework allows practitioners to work collaboratively with the men using straight-talk (that creates relevance, belief in their capacity and honesty/directness) to address the challenges that threaten their relationships.

Since contemporary fathering specifically is increasingly diverse and more complex than it was three decades ago, family-based and community services would benefit greatly by focussing on father presence and its benefits. Men's health campaigns and relationship programs work more effectively and attract wider interest when they build on generative connections in men's lives.

Appendix:

Tips and suggestions

Appendix A

Messages for mothers and fathers

Key messages regarding what mothers can do to support father involvement...

- Discuss expectations of your roles as parents with your partner.
- "Invite dads in" – men have only a short history of being day-to-day nurturers of children. It's possible that their dads were busy working and had little time to share some of the child-rearing responsibilities that come with having a baby. Talk to him about the tasks, issues, needs and your perspective on how to best raise your children.
- Allow fathers to get involved. Sometimes mothers need to hand over control of the baby to fathers so they experience – 'the buck stops with me phenomena' e.g. trust the father to develop the responsibility and capacity to do the nappy changing or baby bathing. Encourage the father to spend time alone with his child. This will really help him to develop his own skills, confidence and ability to nurture your children. This aspect is critical as research shows that many fathers spend less than 30 minutes a week alone with their child in his/her first year of life.

- Discuss parenting by negotiating the child-rearing tasks and house-hold duties to ensure that both your emotional and practical needs are met. Men are very task oriented and more capable of providing support when they know exactly what is expected of them.
- Encourage health professionals to engage with the father. If fathers get the message from both the mother and the health practitioner, then they are more likely to understand the importance of their role in their child's development.

Key messages regarding what fathers with babies can do deepen their involvement...

- Babies enjoy being held, cuddled and gently massaged.
- Babies like it when you talk, sing and play with them.
- Babies like to be comforted, to feel safe and loved.
- Have special time with your baby – organise a regular special time for you and your baby to get to know each other, to strengthen your bond and relationship e.g. go for a walk, go shopping, have a nap together, play.
- The added advantage is that it can free your partner to have some time for herself.
- Learn to fold and change nappies.
- Record your baby's development.
- Learn to bath your baby.
- Hold your baby in a way that is comfortable for you. Remember to support your baby's head as you pick him/ her up.
- Find some way to be involved in feeding your baby.
- Crying is your baby's way of communicating to you – letting you know their needs and feelings. They may be hungry, have a dirty nappy or wind, feeling cold/ hot, tired or may simply want to be held. Comfort your baby. You cannot spoil your baby by giving him/ her too much love.
- Babies and young children need you to protect them from harm. Start by making sure your baby's environment is safe – house, car, bassinette, cot, stroller and toys.
- Find some time alone without the baby. You will need time to reflect on your changed life and new perspectives. It is important to give yourself that time.

- Find some time alone with your partner.
- Do things as a family.
- Be the father you would like to be.

Key messages regarding what fathers with young children can do deepen their involvement ...

- Make time to be a dad: Don't simply assume that you'll have time to be involved with your child. Plan and schedule time to play and talk with your son/daughter
- Be a good role model: Your child watched everything you do and learns how to act and react from your actions. Show him/her the best way to eventually parent their children, by being a great parent yourself.
- Playtime: Playing games with your child is good for both of you and creates a bond between you.
- Teach respect: Especially your boys. They need to learn respect for other males and women in their lives.
- Talk, talk, talk: to your partner, family, friends and health professionals about parenting. This helps create a support network that will "share the parenting load" for you.
- Be a mentor: help other dads become the great dads that they want to become. Share your experiences and expertise with the men around you. This includes your own father. It's never too late to learn.
- Change or improve your household behaviour: Having a baby increases the extent of the household chores unbelievably. Don't expect your partner to do all the extra work. Discuss housework with your partner and make sure that you do your share. TRUST ME – it's well researched and agreed that "the fastest way to a woman's' heart is via the vacuum cleaner and kitchen sink".
- Work together as a team and share all the tasks including housework and breastfeeding.
- Support and respect the mother of your child.
- Spend time ALONE with your children.
- Love your children and show them your affection and encouragement.
- Communicate with your partner, kids and health professionals. Be open with your feelings.
- Spend as much time together as a family as possible having fun and

relaxing. It might be a good time to get closer to your own father too!
* Share your own life story with your children. They need to know and understand who you are.

Key messages for a father to consider to deepen their generative connections as a father...

* What kind of dad would I like to be?
* What sort of relationship would I like with my children? Share your thoughts with your partner about this.
* What kind of memories do I want my child to have about his/her childhood?
* How do I want my child to feel while growing up?
* Have a look at the other priorities in your life and consider whether they are compatible with your new life and your partner's expectations of fatherhood?
* Make time to share fun, enjoyable or pleasant activities with your partner
* Make time to discuss important issues.
* Share your thoughts and feelings (i.e. hopes and dreams, concerns, desires, problems…) with your partner.
* Discover the things that communicate caring. Ask your partner to make a list of ten things that she feels would be an expression of caring from you to her. Spend some time yourself making a similar list. Swap lists and discuss their contents.
* Do at least one thing each day that is an expression of caring for each other.
* Find a way to show your partner that you love them. This could be romantic and affectionate or even cleaning up the kitchen.
* Focus on your shared dreams for your child and family.
* Spend time engaging in pleasant activities as a family.

Appendix B

A family sculpture representation for practitioners to CALD men use using chairs to discuss family role changes.

Below is an excellent exercise to facilitate with large groups of CALD men from different nationalities. It is assumed that each cultural group would have an interpreter, so the concepts need to be clear and simple. The use of the chairs throughout this discussion is a multisensory tool that deepens the men's engagement to the topic. The purpose of the exercise is to discuss the challenges of developing a teamwork parenting approach with their partner. It explores how the fathering role had changed throughout their flight as a CALD family.

This exercise uses three chairs to represent children and two other chairs to represent the father and the mother. It works brilliantly in making the ideas clear while discussing the problems of authoritarian parenting vs teamwork parenting. A sixth chair can be used to represent who could provide help or other family members involved. The chairs provide a concrete representation of all the key ideas and made the job so much easier for the interpreters. It was a 45-minute talk that went for 60-minutes, however it could easily go for 2 hours.

	Place five chairs in the centre of a large U shape area where the men are seated. The facilitator sits in the end chair (filled dot). From this position, discuss how fathering in Australia has changed in the last fifty years. Highlight that, often as similar to their own country of origin, this was a common family structure in the 1950's where the man was the head of the house. Comment on how this has changed and how it had a lot of negative impacts on the men, women and children. Today, the family structure is primarily different. Ask the men in pairs to discuss in their own language how fathering has changed from their own country to here in Australia. Using the interpreters for feedback, discuss comments in the large group. Discuss the challenge of redefining the word 'respect'. Historically it has been synonymous with the word fear. This needs to change! Respect has nothing to do with fear in all relationships.
	Move the chair out the front to the new position. The facilitator sits in this new position (filled dot). Comment that a lot of men in Australia today say that they 'want to father differently to how they were fathered'. Highlight that this position is about teamwork parenting. Discuss with the group its benefits and challenges. Turn the two adult chairs (at the front) inwards and emphasise that it requires the adults to take time to talk together and have a common plan on how to the children. Discuss the challenges of negotiating this plan, rather than assuming that everyone will behave in a certain way. Emphasise that parents are the most important teachers in their children's lives and as the father, he plays a critical role! Emphasise again what respect means today in relationships and in parenting children.
	Discuss with the men what happens when the parents are emotionally apart due to lack of communication, past expectations or working patterns. Discuss the challenges with this and how the children often take control and may act out in their behaviour or spend a lot of time inside watching TV. Discuss healthy parenting and how the parents can come together to have teamwork parenting discussions. Discuss who in their community can support this.

	Sometimes children, especially in CALD families, have an elevated sense of power. The children can act as if they are in charge since they are at school, exposed to new ideas, have a voice and often speak better English than the parents. Discuss with the men the challenge of maintaining the importance of the parents being in charge. Emphasise the problems with using smacking and yelling to control children's behaviour and how the behaviours just get worse and violence is used by the parents. Emphasise how domestic violence and love are completely opposite. Discuss some alternative parenting strategies that enable the parents to be in charge without using violence.
	The facilitator sits in this new position (filled dot) to represent one of the children. Imagine that the three children are aged 4, 9, 14 years and systematically move across the chairs discussing in the group challenges and opportunities for a child of that age in Australia. Try to ensure a balanced view is discussed where the men have greater empathy in how to talk and respond to a child of that age.
	In a similar way, the facilitator sits in this new position (filled dot) to represent the mother and their partner. Discuss where experience in Australia. Discuss what is importance for her and the importance of supporting her choices. This is an important and challenging discussion. Issues around domestic violence can be discussed exploring the problem of men assuming how she should act and how this is controlling. Also how overt or covert force is used that is abusive.
	Discuss the challenges of family separation that could occur especially if domestic violence occurs in the family. Identify what supports are needed when separation occurs and how his vital role continues even if it changes.
	Ask the men in pairs to discuss in their own language how teamwork parenting could occur with their partner. Using the interpreters for feedback, discuss comments in the large group. Discuss who are other family members who may live in the house and their roles. How is that family role respected while maintaining a teamwork parenting approach with the partner.
	Summarise the key points and learning that has occurred from the discussion. Emphasise the important values they bring to parenting and how these values can be passed onto the next generation.

KEY TERMS
AND DEFINITIONS

Keywords: **Child welfare, Father, Fatherhood, Generativity, Social Work**

Definition of Keywords:

Child Welfare - The child welfare system is a group of public and private services that are focused on ensuring that all children live in safe, permanent and stable environments that support their well-being. In Australia, the child welfare system and legislation is different for each State and Territory.

Father - has come to identify a form of social, rather than biological, relationship. In fact there can be no single concept that encapsulates fathering. For the purpose of this chapter the word father then will pertain to both the social and biological aspects of the term.

Fatherhood - a status attained by having a child and remains unchanged -unless an only child dies. The term fatherhood is used interchangeably with the term fathering which includes, beyond the procreative act itself, all the childrearing roles, activities, duties, and responsibilities that fathers are expected to perform and carry out.

Generativity- Generativity involves the capacity to care for the next generation and demands the ability to give something of yourself to another person.

Social Work - Utilising theories of human behaviour and social systems, social work intervenes at the points where people interact with their environments. Principles of human rights and social justice are fundamental to social work. It is understood that social work in the 21st century is dynamic and evolving, and therefore no definition should be regarded as exhaustive. (International Federation of Social Workers, 2000).

Father Inclusive Practice Logos (with permission)
http://groupworksolutions.com.au/FatherInclusivePractice_logo

ENDNOTES

1   Peterson, G. W., & Steinmetz, S. K. (2000). The diversity of father-
    hood. Marriage & Family Review, 29(4), 315-322. doi: 10.1300/
    J002v29n04_05 p.315

2   Russell, G, Barclay, L, Edgecombe, G, Donovan, J, Habib, G,
    Callaghan, H & Pawson, Q. (1999). Fitting Fathers into families:
    Men and the fatherhood role in contemporary Australia. A report for
    the Commonwealth Department of Family and Community Services.

3   Craig, L., M. K., & Blaxland, M. (2010). Parenthood, policy and
    work-family time in Australia 1992—2006 . Work, Employment and
    Society, 27-45 . doi:10.1177/0950017009353778

4   Kululanga, L., Malata, A., & Chirwa, E. & Sundby, J. (2012). Mala-
    wian fathers' views and experiences of fathers attending the birth of
    their children: A qualitative study. Pregnancy and Childbirth , 12:141;
    pp1-10.

5   Squire, C. (Ed). (2009). The Social Context of Birth (2nd Ed).
    Radcliffe Press, Oxford.

6   Fatherhood Institute. (2007, March 20). Fathers at the birth and
    after: Impact on mothers. Retrieved January 16, 2013, from Father-
    hood   Institute: http://www.fatherhoodinstitute.org/2007/father-
    hood-institute-research-summary-fathers-attending-births/

7   Connolly, L. (2018, January 13). "Dad's the word". Retrieved from
    Gender Indicators, Australia, August 2016: http://www.abs.gov.
    au/ausstats/abs@.nsf/Lookup/by%20Subject/4125.0~August%20
    2016~Media%20Release~Dad%27s%20the%20word%20
    (Media%20Release)~2

8   Russell, G, Barclay, L, Edgecombe, G, Donovan, J, Habib, G,
    Callaghan, H & Pawson, Q. (1999). Fitting Fathers into families:
    Men and the fatherhood role in contemporary Australia. A report for
    the Commonwealth Department of Family and Community Services.

9   Fagan, J. & Palm, G. (2004). Fathers and Early Childhood
    Programmes, Clifton Park, NY: Thomson (Delmar Learning).

10 Pleck, J. & Masciadrelli, B. (2004). 'Paternal involvement by U.S.
    residential fathers: Levels, sources and consequences'. In M.E. Lamb
    (Ed.), The Role of the Father in Child Development, 4th Edition (pp.
    222–271). Hoboken, NJ: Wiley.

11 Department for Education and Skills (DfES). (2007). Every Parent Matters. London: The Stationery Office.

12 Robinson, B. (2001). Fathering from the Fast Lane: Practical Ideas for busy dads, Australia: Finch.

13 Scourfield, J., Maxwell, N., Holland, S., Tolman, R., Sloan, L., Featherstone, B. & Bullock, A. (2011). A feasibility study for a randomised controlled trial of a training intervention to improve the engagement of fathers in the child protection system. London: National Institute for Social Care and Health Research.

14 Cosson, B. & Graham, E. (2012). 'I felt like a third wheel': Fathers' stories of exclusion from the 'parenting team'. Journal of Family Studies, 18(2), 121-129. doi: 10.5172/jfs.2012.18.2-3.121

15 Collier,R. & Sheldon, S. (2008) Fragmenting Fatherhood: A Socio-Legal Study, United Kingdom: Bloomsbury Publishing

16 Haskett, M. E., Marziano, B., & Dover, E. R. (1996). Absence of males in maltreatment research: A survey of recent literature. Child Abuse & Neglect, 20 (12), 1175-1182. doi: 10.1016/S0145-2134(96)00113-5

17 Ghate, D. Shaw, C. & Hazel, N. (2000). Fathers and family centers: Engaging fathers in preventative services. York, UK: York Publishing Services.

18 Fletcher, R., Fairbairn, H., & Pascoe, S. (2003). Fatherhood research in Australia. Newcastle, Australia: The Family Action Centre.

19 Ashley, C. Featherstone, B., Roskill, C., Ryan, M, & White, S. (2006). Fathers Matter: Research findings on fathers and their involvement with social care services, London, Family Rights Group

20 Storhaug, A. S., & Oien, K. (2012). Fathers' encounters with the child welfare service. Children and Youth Services Review, 34, 296–303. doi:10.1016/j.childyouth.2011.10.031

21 Zanoni, L., Warburton, W., Bussey, K., & McMaugh, A. (2013). Fathers as "core business" in child welfare practice and research: An interdisciplinary review. Children and Youth Services Review, 35(7), 1055–1070. doi:10.1016/j.childyouth.2013.04.018

22 Milner, J. (1993). A disappearing act: The differing career paths of fathers and mothers in child protection investigations. Critical Social Policy, 38(38), 48–63. doi:10.1177/026101839301303803

23 Milner, J. (2004). From "disappearing" to "demonised": The effects on men and women of professional interventions based on challenging men who are violent. Critical Social Policy, 24(1), 79–101. doi:10.1177/0261018304241004

24   O' Hagan, K. (1997). The problem of engaging men in child protection work. British Journal of Social Work, 27(1), 25–42. doi:10.1093/oxfordjournals.bjsw.a011194

25   O'Donnell, J. M., Johnson, W. E. Jr, D'Aunno, L. E., & Thornton, H. L. (2005). Fathers in child welfare: Caseworkers' perspectives. Child Welfare, 84, 387–414.

26   Curran, L. (2003). Social work and fathers: Child support and fathering programs. Social Work, 48(2), 219–227. doi:10.1093/sw/48.2.219

27   Gordon, D. M., Watkins, N. D., Walling, S. M., Wilhelm, S., & Rayford, B. S. (2011). Adolescent fathers involved with child protection: Social workers speak! Child Welfare, 90, 95–114.

28   Bunston, W. (2013). What about the fathers? Bringing "dads on board" with their infants and toddlers following violence. Journal of Family Studies, 19(1), 70–79. doi:10.5172/jfs.2013.19.1.70

29   Daniel, B., & Taylor, J. (2001). Engaging with fathers: Practice issues for health and social care. London: Jessica Kingsley.

30   Featherstone, B., Rivett, M., & Scourfield, J. (2007). Working with men: Theory and practice in health and social welfare. London: Sage.

31   Ashley, C., Featherstone, B., Roskill, C., Ryan, M., & White, S. (2006). Fathers matter: Research findings on fathers and their involvement with social care services. London: Family Rights Group

32   O' Hagan, K. (1997). The problem of engaging men in child protection work. British Journal of Social Work, 27(1), 25–42. doi:10.1093/oxfordjournals.bjsw.a011194

33   Featherstone, B. (2006). Why gender matters in child welfare and protection. Critical Social Policy, 26(2), 94–314. doi:10.1177/0261018306062587

34   Fletcher, R., Silberberg, S., & Baxter, R. (2001). Fathers' access to family-related service. Newcastle, Australia: The Family Action Centre.

35   Scourfield, J. (2001). Constructing men in child protection work. Men and Masculinities, 4(1), 70–89. doi:10.1177/1097184X01004001004

36   Maxwell, N., Scourfield, J., Featherstone, B., Holland, S. and Tolman, R. (2012), Engaging fathers in child welfare services: a narrative review of recent research evidence. Child & Family Social Work, 17: 160–169.

37   Craig, L., M. K., & Blaxland, M. (2010). Parenthood, policy and work-family time in Australia 1992—2006 . Work, Employment and Society, 27-45 . doi:10.1177/0950017009353778

38 Winslow, S. (2005). Work-family conflict, gender, and parent-hood, 1977-1997. Journal of Family Issues, 26, 727-755. doi:10.1177/0192513X05277522

39 Nomaguchi, K. (2009). Change in work-family conflict among employed parents between 1977 and 1997. Journal of Marriage and the Family, 71(1), 15–32. doi:10.1111/j.17413737.2008.00577.x

40 Townsend, N. (2002). The package deal: Marriage, work, and father-hood in men's lives. Philadelphia, PA: Temple University Press.

41 Coltrane, S. (1996). Family man: Fatherhood, housework, and gender equity. New York: Oxford Press.

42 Kanter, R. (1977). Work and family in the United States: A critical review and agenda for research and policy. New York, NY: Russell Sage Foundation.

43 Kwek, G (2013, December 30). Miner dies at Fortescue's Christmas Creek Mine in WA. Sydney Morning Herald. Retrieved January 28, 2014, from http://www.smh.com.au/business/mining-and-resources/miner-dies-at-fortescues-christmas-creek-mine-in-wa-20131230-302bo.html#ixzz2rg1Bq900

44 Gallegos, D. (2006). Fly-in fly-out employment: Managing the parenting transitions. Perth, Australia: Centre for Social and Community Research.

45 Taylor, J. C., & Simmonds, J. G. (2009). Family stress and coping in the fly-in fly-out workforce. Australian Community Psychologist, 21(2), 23-36. Retrieved from http://www.groups.psychology.org.au.com/publications/

46 Scourfield, J. (2003). Gender and child protection. London: Palgrave MacMillan.

47 Scourfield, J. (2006). The challenge of engaging fathers in the child protection process.Critical Social Policy, 26(2), 440–449. doi:10.1177/0261018306062594

48 Gordon, D. M., Oliveros, A., Hawes, S. W., Iwamoto, D. K., & Rayford, B. S. (2012). Engaging fathers in child protection services: A review of factors and strategies across ecological systems. Children and Youth Services Review, 34(8), 1399–1417. doi:10.1016/j.childyouth.2012.03.02

49 Collier, S. & Sheldon, S. (2008). Fragmenting fatherhood: A socio-legal study, Oxford: Hart.

50 Lamb, M., & Tamis-LeMonda, C. (2004). The role of the father. In M. E. Lamb (Ed.), The role of the father in child development (4th ed., pp. 222–271). Hoboken, NJ: Wiley.

51 Cabrera, N., Tamis-LeMonda, C. S., Bradley, R. H., Hofferth, S., & Lamb, M. E. (2000). Fatherhood in the 21st century. Child Development, 71(1), 127–136. doi:10.1111/1467-8624.00126

52 Milner, J. (1993). A disappearing act: The differing career paths of fathers and mothers in child protection investigations. Critical Social Policy, 38(38), 48–63. doi:10.1177/026101839301303803

53 Featherstone, B., Rivett, M., & Scourfield, J. (2007). Working with men: Theory and practice in health and social welfare. London: Sage.

54 Robson, S. (2006). Parent perspectives on services and relationships in two English early years centres. Early Child Development and Care,176(5), 443-460

55 Cullen, S. M, Cullen, M. A., Band, S., Davis, L., & Lindsay, G. (2010). Supporting fathers to engage with their children's learning and education: An under-developed aspect of the parent support adviser pilot. British Educational Research Journal, 37(3), 485-500. doi: 10.1080/01411921003786579

56 Collier, S. & Sheldon, S. (2008). Fragmenting fatherhood: A socio-legal study, Oxford: Hart.

57 Scott, D., & Arney, F. (Eds.). (2010). Working with vulnerable families: A partnership approach. New York: Cambridge.

58 Scott, D., & Swain, S. (2002). Confronting cruelty, historical perspectives on child protection. Melbourne: Melbourne University Press.

59 Berlyn, C., Wise, S., & Soriano, G. (2008). Engaging fathers in child and family services: Participation, perceptions and good practice (Occasional Paper No. 22). Sydney: National Evaluation Consortium.

60 Walters, M. (2011). Working with fathers: From knowledge to therapeutic practice. UK: Palgrave Macmillan.

61 Tamis-LeMonda, C., & Cabrera, C. (Eds.). (2002). Handbook of father involvement. Mahway, NJ: Lawrence Erlbaum Associates.

62 Bunston, W. (2013). What about the fathers? Bringing "dads on board" with their infants and toddlers following violence. Journal of Family Studies,19(1), 70–79. doi:10.5172/jfs.2013.19.1.70

63 Scott, K. L., & Crooks, C. V. (2006). Effecting change in maltreating fathers: Critical Principles for intervention planning. Clinical Psychology: Science and Practice, 11(1), doi: 10.1093/clipsy.bph058

64 Featherstone, B., & Fraser, C. (2012). Working with fathers around domestic violence: Contemporary debates. Child Abuse Review, 21(4), 255–263. doi:10.1002/car.2221

65   O'Donnell, J. M., Johnson, W. E. Jr, D'Aunno, L.E., & Thornton, H. L. (2005). Fathers in child welfare: Caseworkers' perspectives. Child Welfare, 84, 387–414. Retrieved from http://www.questia.com/library/p435256/child-welfare

66   O' Hagan, K. (1997). The problem of engaging men in child protection work. British Journal of Social Work, 27(1), 25–42. doi:10.1093/oxfordjournals.bjsw.a011194

67   Featherstone, B. (2009). Contemporary fathers: Theory, policy and practice. Bristol: Policy Press.

68   Brown, L., Callahan, M., Strega, S., Walmsley, C., & Dominelli, L. (2009). Manufacturing ghost fathers: The paradox of father presence and absence in child welfare. Child & Family Social Work, 14(1), 25–34. doi:10.1111/j.13652206.2008.00578.x

69   Featherstone, B. (2010). Writing fathers in but mothers out!!! Critical Social Policy, 30(2), 208–224. doi:10.1177/0261018309358290

70   Ferguson, H., & Hogan, F. (2004). Strengthening families through fathers: Issues for policy and practice in working with vulnerable fathers and their families. Dublin: Department of Social, Community and Family Affairs.

71   Strega, S., Fleet, C., Brown, L., Dominelli, L., Callahan, M., & Walmsley, C. (2008). Connecting father absence and mother blame in child welfare policies and practice. Children and Youth Services Review, 30(7), 705–716. doi:10.1016/j. childyouth.2007.11.012

72   Brown, L., Callahan, M., Strega, S., Walmsley, C., & Dominelli, L. (2009). Manufacturing ghost fathers: The paradox of father presence and absence in child welfare. Child & Family Social Work, 14(1), 25–34. doi:10.1111/j.13652206.2008.00578.x

73   Fleming, J. (2010). The absence of fathers in child and family welfare practice (Doctoral dissertation).Retrieved from http://arrow.monash.edu.au/vital/access/manager/Repository/monash:80105

74   Fleming, J., & King, A. (2010). A road less travelled: Working with men as fathers in family based services. Developing Practice, 26, 40-51. Retrieved from: http://www.acwa.asn.au/developing_practice11.html

75   Fronek, P. (Host). (2013b, March 16). Working with fathers from a strengths perspective: In conversation with Andrew King [Episode 46]. Podsocs. Podcast retrieved November 24, 2013, from http://www.podsocs.com/podcast/workingwith-fathers-from-a-strengths-perspective/

76 Fleming, J. (2010). The absence of fathers in child and family welfare practice, PhD Thesis, Monash University. Faculty of Medicine, Nursing and Health Sciences. Dept. Of Social Work, Victoria, Australia, http://arrow.monash.edu.au/hdl/1959.1/523136

77 Maxwell, N., Scourfield, J., Featherstone, B., Holland, S., & Tolman, R. (2012). Engaging fathers in child welfare services: A narrative review of recent research evidence. Child & Family Social Work, 17(2), 160–169. doi:10.1111/j.13652206.2012.00827.x

78 Walmsley, C., Strega, S., Brown, L., Dominelli L., & Callahan, M. (2009). More than a playmate, less than a co-parent: Fathers in the Canadian BSW curriculum. Canadian Social Work Review, 26, 73–96. Retrieved from http://caswe-acfts.ca/cswr-journal/

79 Berlyn, C., Wise, S., & Soriano, G. (2008). Engaging fathers in child and family services: Participation, perceptions and good practice (Occasional Paper No. 22). Sydney: National Evaluation Consortium.

80 Featherstone, B. (2010). Writing fathers in but mothers out!!! Critical Social Policy, 30(2), 208–224. doi:10.1177/0261018309358290

81 Russell, G., & Hwang, C. (2004).The impact of workplace practices on father involvement. In M. Lamb (Ed.), The role of the father in child development (4th ed.). New York: John Wiley & Sons.

82 Fronek, P. (2013, February 2). Involving fathers: In conversation with Joseph Fleming [Episode 42]. Podsocs. Podcast retrieved November 18, 2013, from http://www.podsocs.com/podcast/involving-fathers/

83 Walmsley, C., Strega, S., Brown, L., Dominelli, L, & Callahan, M. (2009). More than a playmate, less than a co-parent: Fathers in the Canadian BSW Curriculum. Canadian Social Work Review / Revue canadienne de service social 26(1), 73-96.

84 Collier, S. & Sheldon, S. (2008). Fragmenting fatherhood: A socio-legal study, Oxford: Hart.

85 Cowan P. A., Cowan, C. P, Pruett, M. K., Pruett, K., & Wong J. J. (2009). Promoting fathers' engagement with children: Preventive interventions for low-income families. Journal of Marriage and the Family, 71, 663–679. doi: 10.1111/j.1741-3737.2009.00625.

86 Bowlby, J. (1988). A secure base: Clinical applications of attachment theory, London: Routledge.

87 Pruett, K. (1987). The Nurturing Father, New York: Warner Books.

88 Berk, L. (2006). 'Emotional Development', Child Development (7th ed.). p 428-429 Boston: Pearson Publishing.

89   Schore, A. (2001). Effects of a Secure Attachment Relationship on Right Brain Development, Affect Regulation, and Infant Mental Health. Association for Infant Mental Health, Vol. 22(1–2), 7–66.

90   Glaser, D. (2000). Child Abuse and Neglect and the Brain–A Review. Journal of Child Psychology and Psychiatry, 97-116.

91   Cabrera, N., & Tamis-LeMonda, C. (2013). Handbook of Father Involvement: Multidisciplinary Perspectives. Routledge.

92   Bogels, S., & Phares, V. (2008). Fathers' role in the etiology, prevention and treatment of child anxiety: A review and new model. Clinical Psychology Review (28), 539-558.

93   Sarkadi, A., Kristiansson, R., Oberklaid, F., & Bremberg, S. (2007). Fathers' Involvement and Children's Developmental Outcomes: A Systematic Review of Longitudinal Studies. Acta Paediatrica, 153–158.

94   Fletcher, R. (2011). The Dad Factor: How the Father-Baby Bond Helps a Child for Life, Finch Publishing, Warriewood, NSW.

95   Lamb, M. E. (1977). Father–infant and mother–infant interaction in the first year of life. Child Development, 48, 167–181.

96   Paquette, D. (2004). Theorizing the Father-Child Relationship: Mechanisms and Developmental Outcomes. Human Development, 193–219. doi:10.1159/000078723

97   Paquette, D. (2004). 'Theorizing the father–child relationship: Mechanisms and developmental outcomes'. Human Development, 47, 193–219.

98   Paquette, D. (2004). Theorizing the father–child relationship: Mechanisms and developmental outcomes. Human Development, 47, 193–219.

99   Fletcher, R. (2011). The Dad Factor: How the Father-Baby Bond Helps a Child for Life, Finch Publishing, Warriewood, NSW.

100 Sethna, V., Murray, L., Edmondson, O., Iles, J., & Ramchandani, P. G. (2018). Depression and playfulness in fathers and young infants: A matched design comparison study. Journal of Affective Disorders, 229, 364-370. doi:https://doi.org/10.1016/j.jad.2017.12.107

101 Allen, S.M. and K.J. Daly, The effects of father involvement: An updated research summary of the evidence. 2007: Centre for Families, Work & Well-Being, University of Guelph.

102 Harbin, S. Julie (2016). Gender Differences in Rough and Tumble Play Behaviours. International Journal of Undergraduate Research and Creative Activities: Vol. 8, Article 5.DOI: http://dx.doi.org/10.7710/2168-0620.1080

103 LaFreniere, P. (2013). Children's play as a context for managing physiological arousal and learning emotion regulation. Psychological Topics, 22(2), 183-204.

104 Shulman, C, (2016), Research and Practice in Infant and Early Childhood Mental Health, Children's Well-Being: Indicators and Research 13, DOI 10.1007/978-3-319-31181-4_2

105 Camras, L & Halberstadt, A (2017). Emotional development through the lens of affective social competence. Current Opinion in Psychology, Volume 17, October 2017, Pages 113-117

106 Bogels, S., & Phares, V. (2008). Fathers' role in the etiology, prevention and treatment of child anxiety: A review and new model. Clinical Psychology Review (28), p 542.

107 Yogman, M. (1981). Games fathers and mothers play with their infants. Infant Mental Health Journal. Retrieved from https://onlinelibrary. wiley.com/doi/abs/10.1002/1097-0355%28198124%292%3A4%3 C241%3A%3AAID-IMHJ2280020406%3E3.0.CO%3B2-8

108 Parke, R., & Sawin, D. (1976). The Father's Role in Infancy: A Re-Evaluation . The Family Coordinator, Vol. 25, No. 4, 365-371.

109 Fatherhood Institute. (2007, March 20). Fathers at the birth and after: Impact on mothers. Retrieved January 16, 2013, from Fatherhood Institute: http://www.fatherhoodinstitute.org/2007/fatherhood-institute-research-summary-fathers-attending-births/

110 Anderson, B.J., & Standley, K. (1976). A methodology for observation of the childbirth experience. Paper presented at the meeting of the American Psychological Association, Washington, D.C.

111 Henneborn, W.J., & Cogan, R. (1975). The effect of husband participation in reported pain and the probability of medication during labor and birth. Journal of Psychosomatic Research, 19, 215-222.

112 Gibbins, J., & Thomson, A. M. (2001). Women's expectations and experiences of childbirth. Midwifery, 17(4), 302-313.

113 Tarkka, M.J,, Paunonen, M., & Laippala, P. (2000). Importance of the midwife in the first-time mother's experience of childbirth. Scandinavian Journal of Caring Science, 14, 184–190.

114 Enkin, M.W., Kierse, M.J.N.C., Renfrew, M., & Neilson, J., with the editorial assistance of Enkin, E. (1995). A Guide to Effective Care In Pregnancy and Childbirth, (2nd ed.). Oxford: Oxford University Press.

115 Mercer, R.T., Hackley, K., & Bostrom, A. (1984). Relationship of the birth experience to later mothering behaviors. Journal of Nurse Midwifery, 30, 204–11.

116 Kululanga, L., Malata, A., & Chirwa, E. & Sundby, J. (2012). Malawian fathers' views and experiences of fathers attending the birth of their children: A qualitative study. Pregnancy and Childbirth , 12:141; pp.1-10.

117 Fatherhood Institute. (2007, March 20). Fathers at the birth and after: Impact on mothers. Retrieved January 16, 2013, from Fatherhood Institute: http://www.fatherhoodinstitute.org/2007/fatherhood-institute-research-summary-fathers-attending-births/

118 Holopainen, D. (2002). The experience of seeking help for postnatal depression. Australian Journal of Advanced Nursing, 19(3), 39-44.

119 Burgess, A. (2010, August 10). Fathers and Postnatal Depression. Retrieved January 17, 2013, from Fatherhood Institute: http://www.fatherhoodinstitute.org/2010/fatherhood-institute-research-summary-fathers-and-postnatal-depression

120 Misri, S., Kostaras, X., Fox, D, & Kostaras, D. (2000). The impact of partner support in the treatment of postpartum depression. Canadian Journal of Psychiatry, 45(6), 554-8.

121 Grube, M. (2004). Pre- and post-partal psychiatric disorders and support from male partners. A first qualitative approximation. Nervenarzt, 75(5), 483-488.

122 Matthey, S., Kavanagh, D. J., Howie, P., Barnett, B., & Charles, M. (2004). Prevention of postnatal distress or depression: an evaluation of an intervention at preparation for parenthood classes. Journal of Affective Disorders, 79(1-3), 113-26.

123 Burgess, A., & Goldman, R. (2018). Who's the bloke in the room? - Fathers during pregnancy and at the birth in the UK. London: Fatherhood Institute.

124 Kaufman, G. (2018). Barriers to equality: why British fathers do not use parental leave. Community, Work & Family, 21(3), 310-325.

125 McAllister, F. & Burgess, A. (2011). Fatherhood: Parenting Programmes and Policy - A Critical Review of Best Practice. Retrieved January 16, 2013, from Fatherhood Institute: http://www.fatherhoodinstitute.org/wp-content/uploads/2012/07/Van-Leer-Fatherhood-Executive-Summary.pdf

126 Månsdotter, A., & Lundin, A. (2010). How do masculinity, paternity leave, and mortality associate? -A study of fathers in the Swedish parental & child cohort of 1988/89. doi:10.1016/j.socscimed.2010.05.008

127 Burgess, A. (2009). Fathering and parenting interventions: What works? London: Fatherhood Institute.

128 South Australian Department of Education and Children's Services. (2010). Engaging fathers: A report of the Fatherhood engagement research Project 2009-2010. Adelaide: Government of South Australia.

129 Kemal Tekin, A. (2012). Father Involvement in Early Childhood Education. International Conference on Educational Research (ICER). Khon Kaen, Thailand: Researchgate . doi:10.13140/2.1.4349.8883

130 Burgess, A. (1998). Fatherhood Reclaimed-the making of the modern father. Sydney : Random House. & Farrell, A.(2001). Father and Child Reunion. Sydney: Finch Publishing.

131 Sarkadi, A., Kristiansson, R., Oberklaid F., Bremberg S. (2008) Fathers' involvement and children's developmental outcomes: A systematic review of longitudinal studies. Acta Paediatr. 97(2):153-158.

132 Cabrera, N., Shannon J., Tamis-LeMonda, C. (2007) Fathers' influence on their children's cognitive and emotional development: from toddlers to Pre-K. Applied Development Science. 11(4):208-213.

133 Wilson K, Prior, M. Father involvement and child well-being. (2011) Journal of Paediatrics and Child Health.47(7):405-407

134 Booth, A.; Scott, M. & King, V. (2009). Father Residence and Adolescent Problem Behavior - Are Youth always better off in two-parent families. Journal of Family Issues , pp.585-605.

135 Paquette, D. (2004). Theorizing the father–child relationship: Mechanisms and developmental outcomes. Human Development, 47, 193–219. doi:10.1159/000078723

136 Hawkins, A., & Dollahite, D. (1997). Generative fathering: Beyond deficit perspectives. California: Sage Publications.

137 Hawkins, A., & Dollahite, D. (1997). Generative fathering: Beyond deficit perspectives. California: Sage Publications.

138 Russell, G, Barclay, L, Edgecombe, G, Donovan, J, Habib, G, Callaghan, H & Pawson, Q. (1999). Fitting Fathers into families: Men and the fatherhood role in contemporary Australia. A report for the Commonwealth Department of Family and Community Services.

139 Wilkins, R., & Lass, I. (2018). The Household, Income and Labour Dynamics in Australia Survey: Selected Findings from Waves 1 to 16. Melbourne: Melbourne Institute: Applied Economic & Social Research.

140 Wilkins, R., & Lass, I. (2018). The Household, Income and Labour Dynamics in Australia Survey: Selected Findings from Waves 1 to 16. Melbourne: Melbourne Institute: Applied Economic & Social Research.

141 Australian Bureau of Statistics (2009). Australian Social Trends, http://www.abs.gov.au/AUSSTATS/abs@.nsf/Lookup/4102.0Main+Features40March%202009

142 Hawkins, A., & Dollahite, D. (1997). Generative fathering: Beyond deficit perspectives. California: Sage Publications.

143 McCashen, W. (2017). The Strengths Approach: Sharing Power, Building Hope, Creating Change. Bendigo: Innovative Resources.

144 Hawkins, A. J., & Dollahite, D. C. (1997). *Generative fathering: Beyond deficit perspectives.* Thousand Oaks, CA: Sage, p.10.

145 Hawkins, A. J., & Dollahite, D. C. (1997). Generative fathering: Beyond deficit perspectives.Thousand Oaks, CA: Sage.

146 Hawkins, A. J., & Dollahite, D. C. (1997). Generative fathering: Beyond deficit perspectives.Thousand Oaks, CA: Sage., p.30

147 O'Brien, C & Rich, K 2002, Evaluation of the Men and Family Relationships Initiative–*Final and Supplementary Report*, Commonwealth Department of Family and Community Services, Canberra.

148 http://health.gov.au/malehealthpolicy

149 King, A. (2018) Continual Change Groupwork. Groupwork Solutions, Sydney

150 Cowan, P.A.., Cowan, C.P., Pruett, M.K., Pruett, K., & Wong, J.J. (2009). Promoting fathers' engagement with children: Preventive interventions for low-income families. Journal of Marriage and Family 71 (3), 663-77.

151 Allen, S. and Daly, K. (2007). The effects of father involvement: An updated research summary of the evidence inventory. Centre for Families, Work, and Wellbeing: University of Guelph.

152 Pruett, K. (2000). Father-need, New York; Broadway Books.

153 Garfield, C. & Fletcher, R. (2001). 'Sad Dads: A Challenge for Pediatrics', Pediatrics, Vol. 127, No. 4, pp 781-782.

154 Doherty, W. , Kouneski, E. & Erickson, M. (1998). 'Responsible fathering: An overview and conceptual framework'. Journal of Marriage and the Family, 60(2), 277-293.

155 Colling, T 1992, Beyond Mateship–Understanding Australian Men, Simon & Schuster, Sydney.

156 O'Brien, C & Rich, K 2002, Evaluation of the Men and Family Relationships Initiative– *Final and Supplementary Report*, Commonwealth Department of Family and Community Services, Canberra.

157 Nixon, M (Hon) 1999, Report of the Committee Reviewing Family and Parent *Support Services for Men*. WA.

158 Tehan, B., & McDonald, M. (2010). Engaging fathers in child and Family services. Canberra: Communities and families Clearinghouse Australia.

159 King, A. (2000). Working with fathers: The non-deficit perspective. Children Australia, Vol 25, No.3.

160 King, A. Sweeney, S & Fletcher, R. (2004). A Checklist for Organisations Working with Men. Developing Practice, Number 11, Summer.

161 King, A. Sweeney, S & Fletcher, R. (2004). A Checklist for Organisations Working with Men. Developing Practice, Number 11, Summer.

162 Burgess, A. (2009). Fathering and parenting interventions: What works? London: Fatherhood Institute.

163 Burgess, A. (2009). Fathering and parenting interventions: What works? London: Fatherhood Institute.

164 Tehan, B., & McDonald, M. (2010). Engaging fathers in child and Family services. Canberra: Communities and families Clearinghouse Australia.

165 Sanders, A., Oates, R., & Kahn, T. (2010). Hard to reach? Engaging fathers in early years settings. University of Derby.

166 Bulletin, A. F. (2013). Fatherhood Research Bulletin. Newcastle: University of Newcastle. January.

167 Cowan, C., Cowan, P., Pruett, M., & Pruett, K. (2005). Working strategies: Encouraging stronger relationships between fathers and children. USA: Family Resource Centres. Vol.8; Issue 4, Summer.

168 Fletcher, R. (2012). Men friendly services: Why, what and how. Men Friendly Seminar Evaluation Report (p. 6-21). Penrith: Penrith City Council.

169 Harder, A. 2008, The Developmental Stages of Erik Erikson. www.learningplaceonline.com/stages/organize/Erikson.htm

170 Vaillant, G. 2002, Ageing Well. Little, Brown and Company, New York, p.115

171 Fleming, J. (2002). Just the two of us: The involvement of fathers in building stronger families. Developing Practice; Winter.

172 Hawkins, A. J., & Dollahite, D. C. (1997). Generative fathering: Beyond deficit perspectives. Thousand Oaks, CA: Sage, p.18

173 Palkovitz, R., & Hull, J. (2018). Toward a Resource Theory of Fathering. Journal of Family Theory and Review, 181-195. doi:10.1111/jfr.12239

174 Vaillant, G. 2002, Ageing Well. Little, Brown and Company, New York

175 Agano, M., Friend, K., Tonigan, S., & Stout, R. (2004). Helping other alcoholics in Alcoholics Anonymous and drinking outcomes: Findings from project MATCH. Journal of studies on alcohol, 766-773.

176 Zvara, B. J., Schoppe-Sullivan, S. J., & Kamp Dush, C. (2013). Fathers' involvement in child health care: Associations with prenatal involvement, parents' beliefs, and maternal gatekeeping. Family Relations, 62(4), 649-661. doi: 10.1111/fare.12023

177 Brotherson, S., Dollahite, D., & Hawkins, A. (2005). Generative Fathering and the Dynamics of Connection between Fathers and Their Children. Fathering, 3(1), 1-28.

178 Snarey, J. (1993). How fathers care for the next generation: A four decade study. Cambridge, MA: Harvard University Press.

179 Snarey, J. (1993). How fathers care for the next generation: A four decade study. Cambridge, MA: Harvard University Press.

180 Hawkins, & Dollahite 1997, Generative fathering: Beyond deficit perspectives, Sage Publications, California.

181 Robinson, B. (2001). Fathering from the fast lane: Practical ideas for busy dads. Australia: Finch.

182 Australian Bureau of Statistics.(2011b). Family characteristics, Australia,2009–10 (Cat.No.4442.0).Canberra: ABS. Retrieved from tinyurl.com/k3hnqj8.

183 Smyth, B. (2004) 'Post-separation fathering: What does Australian research tells us?', Journal of Family Studies, Vol. 10, No.1, 20-49.

184 Kaspiew, R., De Maio, J., Qu, L., & Deblaquiere, J. (2014). Post-separation parenting arrangements involving minimal time with one parent In A. Hayes & D. Higgins (Eds.), Families, policy and the law: Selected essays on contemporary issues for Australia. Melbourne: Australian Institute of Family Studies.

185 Kaspiew, R., De Maio, J., Qu, L., & Deblaquiere, J. (2014). Post-separation parenting arrangements involving minimal time with one parent In A. Hayes & D. Higgins (Eds.), Families, policy and the law: Selected essays on contemporary issues for Australia. Melbourne: Australian Institute of Family Studies.

186 Kaspiew, R., De Maio, J., Qu, L., & Deblaquiere, J. (2014). Post-separation parenting arrangements involving minimal time with one parent In A. Hayes & D. Higgins (Eds.), Families, policy and the law: Selected essays on contemporary issues for Australia. Melbourne: Australian Institute of Family Studies.

187 Smyth, B. (2004) 'Post-separation fathering: What does Australian research tells us?', Journal of Family Studies, Vol. 10, No.1, 20-49.

188 Kruk, E. (1993) Divorce and disengagement: Patterns of fatherhood within and beyond marriage. Fernwood Publishing, Halifax.

189 Smyth, B. (2004) 'Post-separation fathering: What does Australian research tells us?', Journal of Family Studies, Vol. 10, No.1, 20-49.

190 Smyth, B. (2004) 'Post-separation fathering: What does Australian research tells us?', Journal of Family Studies, Vol. 10, No.1, 20-49.

191 Altobelli, T. (2006) 'Parenting after separation: The Family Law Amendment (Shared Parental Responsibility) Act 2006', Law Society Journal, Vol. 44, No.6, July, 47-49.

192 Kruk, E. (1993) Divorce and disengagement: Patterns of fatherhood within and beyond marriage. Fernwood Publishing, Halifax.

193 Killeen, D. with Lehmann, J. (2004) 'Non-residential fathers and their support needs',Children Australia, Vol 29, No 5, pp. 12–19

194 Kruk, E. (1993) Divorce and disengagement: Patterns of fatherhood within and beyond marriage. Fernwood Publishing, Halifax.

195 Kruk, E. (1993) Divorce and disengagement: Patterns of fatherhood within and beyond marriage. Fernwood Publishing, Halifax.

196 Killeen, D. with Lehmann, J. (2004) 'Non-residential fathers and their support needs',Children Australia, Vol 29, No 5, pp. 12–19

197 Hawkins, A. J., & Dollahite, D. C.(1997). Generative fathering: Beyond deficit perspectives. Thousand Oaks, CA: Sage

198 Smyth, B. (2004) 'Post-separation fathering: What does Australian research tells us?', Journal of Family Studies, Vol. 10, No.1, 20-49.

199 Hawkins, A. J., & Dollahite, D. C. (1997). Generative fathering: Beyond deficit perspectives. Thousand Oaks, CA: Sage

200 Bryan, M. (1997) The Prodigal Father, Three Rivers Press, USA

201 Smyth, B. (2004) 'Post-separation fathering: What does Australian research tells us?', Journal of Family Studies, Vol. 10, No.1, 20-49.

202 Bryan, M. (1997) The Prodigal Father, Three Rivers Press, USA.

203 Bryan, M. (1997) The Prodigal Father, Three Rivers Press, USA.

204 Bryan, M. (1997) The Prodigal Father, Three Rivers Press, USA.

205 Bryan, M. (1997) The Prodigal Father, Three Rivers Press, USA.

206 Killeen, D. with Lehmann, J. (2004) 'Non-residential fathers and their support needs',Children Australia, Vol 29, No 5, pp. 12–19

207 Smyth, B. (2004) 'Post-separation fathering: What does Australian research tells us?', Journal of Family Studies, Vol. 10, No.1, 20-49.

208 Fletcher, R. (n.d.). Bringing fathers in handbook: How to engage with men for the benefit of everyone in the family: The engaging fathers project, Family Action Centre, University of Newcastle.

209 Children's Trust Fund. (2004). The fatherhood kit: Promoting the positive involvement of fathers in their children's lives. Boston: Massachusetts Children's Trust Fund.

210 Dollahite, D., Slife, B., & Hawkins, A. (1998). Dollahite, Family Generativity and Generative Counseling: Helping families keep faith with the next generation. In M. D. (Eds), Generativity and adult development: How and why We Care for the Next Generation (pp. 449-481). Washington DC: American Psychological Association.

211 Hornby, G. (1992). A review of fathers' accounts of their experiences of parenting children with disabilities. Disability, Handicap and Society, 7(4), 363-374.

212 Hovey, J. K. (2005). Fathers parenting chronically ill children: Concerns and coping strategies. Issues in Comprehensive Pediatric Nursing, 28, 83-95.

213 Esdaile, S. A., & Greenwood, K. M. (2003). A comparison of mothers' and fathers' experience of parenting stress and attributions for parent-child interaction outcomes. Occupational Therapy International, 10(2), 115-126.

214 Esdaile, S. A., & Greenwood, K. M. (2003). A comparison of mothers' and fathers' experience of parenting stress and attributions for parent-child interaction outcomes. Occupational Therapy International, 10(2), 115-126.

215 Simmerman, S., Blacher, J., & Baker, B. L. (2001). Fathers' and mothers' perceptions of father involvement in families with young children with a disability. Journal of Intellectual and Developmental Disability, 26(4), 325-338.

216 King, G., Stewart, D., King, S., & Law, M. (2000). Organizational characteristics and issues affecting the longevity of self-help groups for parents of children with special needs. Qualitative Health Research, 10(2), 225-241.

217 Contact a Family. (2006). Attracting and keeping members. Retrieved 20 August 2006, from www.cafamily.org.uk

218 Dollahite, D., Slife, B., & Hawkins, A. (1998). Dollahite, Family Generativity and Generative Counseling: Helping families keep faith with the next generation. In M. D. (Eds), Generativity and adult development: How and why We Care for the Next Generation (pp. 449-481). Washington DC: American Psychological Association.

219 Government of Western Australia. (2015). Freedom from Fear: Working towards the elimination of family and domestic violence in Western Australia. Perth: Department for Child Protection and Family Support.

220 Donovan, R., Paterson, D., & Francas, M. (199). Targeting male perpetrators of intimate partner violence: Western Australia's "Freedom from Fear" campaign. Retrieved from PubMed: https://www.ncbi.nlm.nih.gov/pubmed/12322576

221 Donovan, R., Paterson, D., & Francas, M. (199). Targeting male perpetrators of intimate partner violence: Western Australia's "Freedom from Fear" campaign. Retrieved from PubMed: https://www.ncbi.nlm.nih.gov/pubmed/12322576

222 Bancroft, L., & Silverman, J. (2002). The Batterer as Parent: Addressing the Impact of Domestic Violence on Family Dynamics. Thousand Oaks, CA: Sage.

223 Fox, G., & Benson, M. (2004). Violent men, bad dads? Fathering profiles of men involved in intimate partner violence. In R. Day, & M. Lamb, Conceptualizing and measuring father involvement. Mahwah, New Jersey: Lawrence Erlbaum Associates Publishers.

224 Stanley, N. (2009). Men's Talk: Tackling Domestic Violence. Summary of the presentation (pp. 1-32). Cardith: Gender and Child Welfare Network.

225 Perel, G., & Peled, E. (2008). The fathering of violent men: Constriction and yearning. Violence against women Journal Vol.14 No. 4 April .

226 Perel, G., & Peled, E. (2008). The fathering of violent men: Constriction and yearning. Violence against women Journal Vol.14 No. 4 April .

227 Perel, G., & Peled, E. (2008). The fathering of violent men: Constriction and yearning. Violence against women Journal Vol.14 No. 4 April .

228 Anderson, H., & Goolishian, H. (1992). The client is the expert: A not-knowing approach to therapy. In S. McNamee & K. J. Gergen (Eds.), Inquiries in social construction. Therapy as social construction (pp. 25-39). Thousand Oaks, CA, US: Sage Publications, Inc.

229 Anderson, H., & Goolishian, H. (1992). The service user is the expert: A not-knowing approach to therapy. In S. McNamee, & K. Gergen, Therapy as Social Construction. London: Sage.

230 Kaplan, I. (1998). Rebuilding Shattered Lives. Melbourne: Victorian Foundation for Survivors of Torture.

www.ingramcontent.com/pod-product-compliance
Lightning Source LLC
Chambersburg PA
CBHW032145020426
42334CB00016B/1235